University Architecture

Brian Edwards

University Architecture

London and New York

First published 2000
by Spon Press
11 New Fetter Lane, London EC4P 4EE

Simultaneously published in the USA and Canada
by Spon Press
29 West 35th Street, New York, NY 10001

Spon Press is an imprint of the Taylor & Francis Group

Typeset in 9.5/12pt Helvetica 45 by Fox Design, Godalming, Surrey
Printed in Great Britain by Bell & Bain Ltd Glasgow

British Library Cataloguing in Publication Data
A catalogue record for this book is available from the British Library

Library of Congress Cataloging in Publication Data

Edwards, Brian, 1944-
University architecture / Brian Edwards.
p. cm.
Includes bibliographical references and index.
ISBN 0-419-24470-0 (pbk.)
1. College buildings. 2. Campus planning. 1. Title

NA6600 .E34 2000
727'.3--dc21

00-032228

Contents

Acknowledgements

My chief acknowledgement is to the many architects whose work I have used to construct the argument that campuses matter. There are too many to list but I would single out for their courteous and enthusiastic support: Jourda and Perraudin, Foster and Partners, MacCormac Jamieson Prichard, Richard Rogers Partnership, Feilden Clegg and, finally, Edward Cullinan and Partners.

I am also greatly indebted to many universities who tirelessly provided plans and responded to my detailed inquiries. Special thanks go to the Universities of London, Cambridge, Glasgow and Edinburgh in the UK; to the Universities of Virginia, Michigan, Ohio, Davis, Berkeley and Stanford in the USA; the University of British Columbia in Canada; Cape Town University in South Africa and the University of Marne-La-Vallée in France.

Finally, the author is particularly indebted to Susan Ellis at the Academic Typing Service, University of Huddersfield, who typed and corrected many manuscripts, without a hint of complaint. Also thanks to Professor Brian Carter from the University of Michigan for his help with last minute queries.

Introduction

In his *A History of Building Types* (1976) Nikolaus Pevsner inexplicably ignores the university as a specific category of building. He defines the library, town hall, railway station and fourteen other building types as having their own distinctive taxonomy of form, yet the university is ignored. This is perhaps because the university is essentially a place where various types of building are located in an ordered relationship. Pevsner, no doubt, saw the university as consisting of its own interpretation of more familiar typologies – the senate house analogous with the town hall, the laboratory with the factory, the university library with the library in general.

Few students and academics today would not recognise the university as a distinctive place with its own blend of buildings, spaces and landscaped gardens. The campus, as we increasingly refer to this environment, has a flavour all of its own. The key elements of university character are forged not only by buildings and landscape, but by people and activity. It is the students engaged in discussion or hurrying to the next lecture which help define a university's sense of place. That is why urban space and urban landscaping are so important to university identity. Enclosure, route, gateway, promenade and vista are essential qualities in campus place making.

But universities have a higher mission too, and this gives the design of buildings a cutting edge to which few other areas of architecture aspire. It is the fashioning of a dialogue through bricks and mortar, or more likely steel and glass, with intellectual mission in the broadest sense. Universities have the almost unique challenge of relating the built fabric to academic discourse. Put another way, the university environment is part of the learning experience and buildings need to be silent teachers. Whether this is achieved through the design of external spaces or via built form depends upon local circumstance, but the principle of academic mission being expressed or explored through the estate of buildings is an important one. And it is this, as much as the external environment, which defines and distinguishes the university.

Universities are places of learning. The ensemble of buildings and spaces we call the modern campus does not easily or naturally establish a sense of place, let alone a sense of an environment of learning or intellectual challenge. The main problem with creating a harmonious campus is the disparate nature of the buildings which make up their composition. The university environment is composed of large buildings, each one often a landmark in its own right. There is little background architecture and few neutral buildings unless significant areas of student housing exist. This makes the modern university campus different from the colleges of old with their pattern of lodgings, halls, masters' rooms, library and refectory.

Creating unity of place out of largely institutional land uses is difficult whether the campus is in the city centre or located on an arcadian site beyond the urban edge. Site planning using large and diverse buildings arranged around service areas and car parks does not lead easily to an attractive campus. Although a masterplan will normally exist, the pressure of change frequently distorts the continuity of intent. Long-lived as the major buildings may be, the speed of change in the world of higher education disrupts orderly growth. The result may be a healthy measure of chaos or richness, or, if change is not well managed, the environment may become disorderly and inefficient.

The character of universities is often a charming dialogue between order and disarray. When strong masterplans exist with clearly structured patterns of buildings and landscape (as at the University of Stanford or the University of Sussex) new interventions can add unexpected richness. Campus character is about recognising and celebrating order, especially in the major buildings, while accepting the intellectual or physical challenge of newcomers.

The structural and spatial units of campus architecture are both large and individual. Whether it be the university library or sports hall, the parts have their own functional logic and service requirements. This gives a distinctive but often inharmonious character to many contemporary universities, especially those which have grown up incrementally (most marked in the UK by universities which started as polytechnics and assumed university status later in life). Here the challenge is one of giving order to disordered campuses, of imposing processional ways and land-use hierarchies upon places without obvious spatial structure.

Part one

The campus

CHAPTER 1

Academic mission and campus planning

Defining a university: the challenge of design

A university may be defined as a self-governing, mainly publicly funded, community of academics and students engaged in absorbing, advancing or disseminating knowledge. Normally a university occupies a well defined physical area, giving it a sense of identity and social focus. There are exceptions, such as the UK's Open University, which relies upon electronic media and summer schools for communicating with students engaged in academic discourse, but generally buildings make a university in both functional and spiritual terms. Since universities are diverse communities of scholars engaged in collective pursuit of knowledge, it is normally necessary to express the academic character of different institutions in built form and spatial pattern. Reinforcing the high ideals of learning through the physical fabric gives architects the opportunity to experiment or innovate. Historically, and particularly over the past fifty years, some of the most challenging and original works of architecture have been for university clients.

1.1 The University of East Anglia, Norwich, UK, has been an important centre for architectural experiment since its foundation in 1965.

Whereas vice-chancellors are keen to express the mission of their university in built form, or the matrix of spaces created, visionary architects are also drawn to the arena of the universities by the climate of invention fostered by academic ideals. Two examples illustrate the argument – Le Corbusier's Carpenter Fine Arts Center at Harvard University (1959–63) and James Stirling's History Faculty Building at Cambridge University (1965–7). Both were for well-established universities and led to buildings of great symbolic weight and volumetric invention constructed within highly conservative physical environments, and each in different ways became the focus for heated debate among academics. The need for new buildings to express or challenge values beyond the utilitarian is arguably the distinguishing feature of the best of university architecture.

Universities in worn out cities are a symbol of physical and intellectual renewal. New universities constructed in

1.2 Engineering Building, Leicester University, UK, by James Stirling (1965).

emerging countries serve a similar spiritual function. Though constructed of concrete, steel and glass, a university is more easily defined in academic than social or architectural terms. We know that universities have high standards of governance and scholarship but these ideals are not always translated into physical environments. One of the best measures of a university is whether it looks like a centre of higher education. Such criteria transcend function and address questions of meaning and identity. This is dangerous territory for chancellors and designers alike, but for a university to fully fulfil its mission, the fabric of education (both buildings and spaces) needs to reflect academic aspirations. A university committed to testing and applying new skills or knowledge should embrace these within the built estate. New concepts in education lead to environments of innovation.

Universities are places of teaching and learning. They generate a feeling of community in whole and in part. The role of colleges is to create small, self-regulating units of resdential scholars who share dining and other social spaces.Sometimes the challenge is not so much that of establishing a distinct character for a college but for a faulty. Here a group of buildings or a single large one may require its own identity in order to reinforce the sense of a distinctive academic community. The administrative structure of a university, whether it be by faculties or colleges (or a combination) provides a framework for architectural expression. The hierarchies of built form, the spatial pattern of campus parts, the order of connection and much else needs to reflect the mission and organisation of the university in the widest sense. Where a university masterplan is based upon flexibility in the assembly of buildings it can lead to loss of environmental distinctiveness and the breakdown of a sense of place for faculties.

The speed of change in research and learning puts great stress upon the notion of academic community. The places created for learning become themselves stressed by the forces of change released by that learning. The striving for innovation in research, scholarship and teaching which universities promulgate creates a momentum of instability which highlights the limit of buildings to contain the activities within them. More than most building types, university teaching departments or research centres are less forms which follow function than those which struggle to contain dynamic uses.

If the speed of change is such that stability of form and function is only achieved for short periods, how then is reconciliation with the feeling of community to be achieved? The answer lies in distinguishing between building types and, in the buildings themselves, between rapid change and permanent elements. Halls of residence are less subject to unpredictable change than research laboratories, for example, and processional or ceremonial spaces (senate room, graduation hall) are less stressed by innovation than teaching or seminar rooms. Handling the forces of change within buildings requires a distinction to be made between the various elements of construction so that parts can be replaced or changed without distorting the whole. For instance, the main structural grid of columns should be free of walls, the walls unencumbered by built-in services, the power supplies free to change without great disruption to finishes and so on. It is an approach to design which gives physical and spatial clarity to the parts, which accepts orders or timescales of change, which allows for the unpredictable at the design stage, and which accepts that the logic of maintenance should influence design.

The degree of change is a measure of the vitality of a university. Institutions which are not perpetually disfigured by tower cranes and construction plants may not be evolving to meet new student demands. Internal change can only meet some of the fresh functions required of educational innovation. Often functional innovation expresses itself in extensions to existing buildings. Research laboratories may have to be expanded to provide space for new scientific processes; successful faculties require additional teaching space; the notion of student-centred learning changes the use, form and content of libraries. Inevitably, academic change is expressed in the fabric of the university and the need to accommodate unpredictable, spasmodic and often rapid change is a frequent requirement of design briefs. The university masterplan has somehow to create a feeling of community among students and lecturers yet provide the means to accommodate change without disruption. The two factors – flexibility and order –

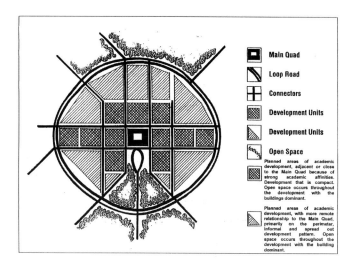

are often in conflict. Cementing the sense of collegiate character requires physical identity and spatial enclosure. Traditionally the college was expressed through the vehicle of the courtyard, more recently the university was built around a processional street or linked squares – London University is a good example of connected squares of learning and Harvard of a pattern of processional streets. In both cases physical enclosure by buildings is the means by which social space is defined. Yet external space is just what expansion and change requires. Just as within buildings space is the means of accommodating flexibility, the same is true of the external environment. Space is required around the perimeter of buildings to meet the relentless pressure for growth on the university campus but to provide such space at the outset undermines the creation of physical enclosure which is the main means by which collegiate character is imparted.

There are models of successful campus masterplans which create a sense of place and accommodate change. Michael Wilford's radially ordered masterplan for Temasek Polytechnic, Singapore (1994), cleverly distinguishes between permanent and less permanent parts, creating space for expansion in a fashion which does not destroy the campus core or undermine teaching territories. The academic centre is well defined in volumetric and external space terms, the linear expansion of different teaching

1.4 Legibility and extendibility combined at Temasek Polytechnic, Singapore, by Michael Wilford and Partners.

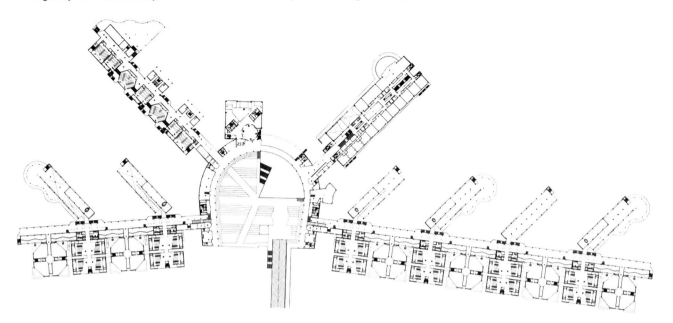

areas can be readily achieved, and the research areas can be altered or redeveloped without great disruption to the remainder. In addition, the campus has a unifying sense of landscape, an order which is planted rather than built, and which addresses the need for reflection within education.

The sense of place helps universities market themselves to potential students. In the competitive world of higher education, architectural quality matters. As students generally visit different universities before making their final choice, the visual impact of the campus is vital. The quality of environment is seen as an important selling point for universities judging by the images used in university prospecti. Most show students busying themselves against a backcloth of modern buildings and friendly external spaces. Some prospecti also show off the latest buildings by fashionable architects (Thames Valley University with its new library by the Richard Rogers Partnership) in the hope of attracting students to the campus.

The marketing of universities through design provides a further justification for the pursuit of architectural quality. If the university does not project a positive image of itself through its built fabric, it is unlikely to attract the best students. Since many universities supplement their income by hosting conferences or attracting business clients, the character of the campus has economic significance here as well. As universities become increasingly business orientated, marketing through architectural image helps raise awareness of the economic value of good design.

Universities are not only a dialogue between academic image and built form in the widest sense, they are also engaged in a discourse with time and space, or, put another way, with history and geography. History shapes cultur-

1.5 Architectural image can help promote a new university. Paul Hamlyn Learning Resource Centre, Thames Valley University, Slough, UK, by Richard Rogers Partnership.

Table 1.1 Types of University Campus

Type	Example	Architect	Advantage	
Place Making: building centred	University of Birmingham University of London	Aston Webb Charles Holden	Strong identity	↑
Place Making: landscape centred	University of Virginia University of California (Berkeley) Technical University of Helsinki	Thomas Jefferson F L Olmsted Alvar Aalto	Strong sense of place, tranquil	15–19th Centuries
Collegiate	University of Cambridge University of Stanford (part)	Various Various	Privacy with local identity	
Linear/megastructure	University of Sussex Simon Fraser University, British Columbia	Basil Spence Erickson and Massey	Extendible, good internal communication	↓
Grid	Illinois Institute of Technology University of North Carolina	Mies van der Rohe Various	Efficient in land utilisation	↑
Modular	University of York Royal University College, London	RMJM E Cullinan and Partners	Economic with visual consistency	
Molecular	University of Sunderland University of Lincoln	Building Design Partnership RMJM	Ordered yet with diversity	20th Century
Radial	Temasek Polytechnic, Singapore	Michael Wilford and Partners	Clarity of route, integration with landscape	
Ad hoc	University of Strathclyde Massachusetts Institute of Technology (MIT)	Various Various	Opportunistic but disordered	↓

al awareness and this, with many nations, is an important factor in determining the layout and detailed planning of universities. A good example is the new university at Qatar, which blends modernity in the form of rectangular buildings with elements of Islamic culture. The campus, designed by Kamal El Kafrawi, has two separate social worlds for male and female students while allowing full intellectual interaction in the lecture theatre or laboratory. The campus also exploits traditional approaches to sun-shading, cooling and ventilation, using wind towers and inter-connected courtyards. The history and geography of place are so well integrated at Qatar University that the campus won an Aga Khan Award for Architecture in 1987. Modernity in the form of universal standards of degree quality and accepted methods of research inquiry is tempered in the best universities by regional cultural currents. Among other benefits, the sense of place provides a reassuring stepping stone for younger nations engaged in the global industry of higher education.

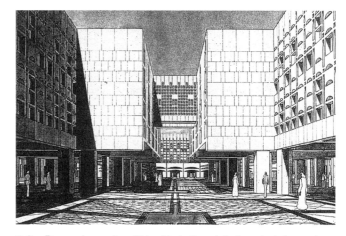

1.6 Preserving cultural identity in the global marketplace of higher education is important. Medical School, King Faisal University, Dammam Saudi Arabia, by Andrautt Parat with Beeah Architects.

6

If a university is defined as a community of scholars engaged in the collective pursuits of knowledge, then questions of community take on academic, social and cultural connotations. Intellectual space – the territory of the mind where learning occurs – has necessarily to engage with social space and to a degree with cultural space, that is space fashioned by a scholar's sense of history and geography. It is one thing to design a university with a feeling of community and operational flexibility, quite another to give it a sense of regional location beyond the pastiche. The problem is exacerbated by the too frequent employment of 'named' architects for university projects anywhere in the world. The want of bedding education into place and time is a common cause of alienation among university students from developing countries. The best university plans balance the creation of abstract space for learning with a strong national identity.

Types of masterplan

It is possible to distinguish nine types of campus plan among the countless university developments across the world. Any classification is, however, frequently compromised by the passage of time. Where a university starts with one type of organising principle it rarely survives the change of ambition of different vice-chancellors or the evolving values of successive generations.

The different campus development paradigms outlined below are a means of achieving the efficient utilisation of land and infrastructure services while giving universities that rare but essential quality – academic character. Different patterns of layout have been popular with certain periods of university development. The college structure is an ancient configuration yet it survives into the twentieth century in the form of the University of York (1960–4) by Robert Matthew, Johnson-Marshall and Partners (RMJM). The megastructure, whereby most teaching departments are housed in a single multi-level spine of accommodation, dates mainly from the last thirty years (eg Simon Fraser University, British Columbia, by Erickson and Massey 1968–72). The use of a park, lawn or garden as a central reflective space for academics from different disciplines grew

up mainly in the Renaissance but found particular expression in Thomas Jefferson's plan for the University of Virginia (1817). It too has been revised in the late twentieth century at the Bothell Campus extension to the University of Washington, Seattle, where the natural environment is brought into close proximity with buildings in order to promote in students an idea of 'stewardship of the land'.[1]

Whatever campus layout is adopted carries formal and academic connotations. Putting aside questions of economics, efficient land utilisation and operational flexibility (a key criteria for site layout) there will inevitably in places of learning be interpretations of meaning around the issue of 'academic character'. The realm of campus planning is rarely made up of simple choices exercised by rational decision makers on the basis of quantifiable data. More frequently judgement is tempered by perceptions of value and cultural association. Environmental stewardship has already been mentioned but campus layout influences attitudes to social behaviour, to academic interaction, to the relative positions of professor and student in the campus pecking order, and to the relationship between the vice-chancellorship and the remainder of the academic community. To allow the choice of masterplan type to be dictated by cost and the needs of future flexibility alone is to abdicate responsibility for fashioning an academic community in the full sense of the term.

The following nine types of masterplan can be identified – *place making: building dominated, place making: landscape dominated, collegiate, linear, grid, modular, molecular, radial* and *ad hoc.* Their main characteristics are as follows.

Place making: building-dominated plans Here there is a strong sense of campus identity forged mainly by the presence of usually large bold buildings. Such campuses are normally near city centres with university buildings grouped around streets or urban squares. Generally, the major university buildings make contributions to the skyline of the area and have a strong presence on the street. This type of campus evolved mainly in the late nineteenth century but had matured into the typical campus of the industrial city by the mid-twentieth century. The universities of Leeds, London and Detroit are all good examples.

1.7   Central campus, University of Michigan, Ann Arbor, USA.

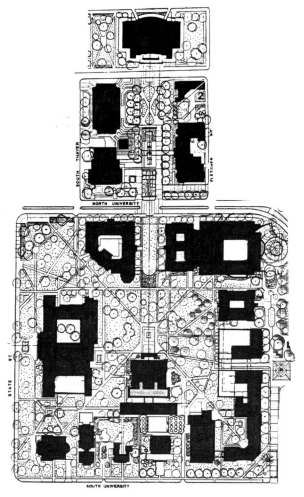

Such campuses today have three main drawbacks: there is little room for expansion, car parking tends to destroy the sense of place and the bustle of city life is not conducive to academic reflection. However, being centrally located, this category of university benefits from good public transport links and can take advantage of other facilities in urban areas for learning such as public libraries and art galleries.

Place making: landscape-dominated plans This type of campus has a sense of place dominated by landscape design. The presence of a backcloth of well planted greenery and sometimes nature in unmanicured form provides

a relaxing and reflective environment for learning. Such campuses evolved on the urban edge or on virgin land and frequently took advantage of sites with special qualities. The wooded hillside at McGill University in Ottawa or the loch-side environment at the University of Stirling in Scotland are typical examples.

Campuses fashioned by the intellectual challenge of nature owe their origins in part to the philosophy of the eighteenth century. Nature and landscape were seen as

1.8   University of Stirling, Scotland, UK, by RMJM.

1.9 Modern interpretation of collegiate character at Chaucer College, University of Kent, UK, by HKPA.

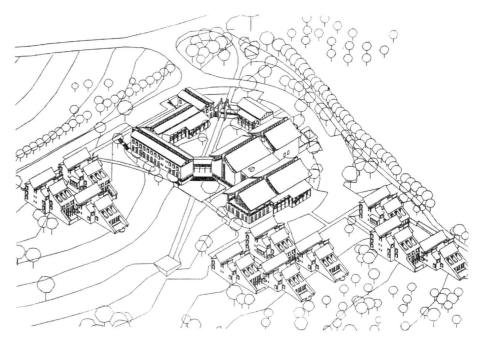

conducive to civilised thought and the value of walks through woods and meadows celebrated as in Frederick Law Olmsted's campus layouts at Stanford and Berkeley. The landscape-dominated campus offers three advantages: the tranquillity feeds creative thought, nature is itself instructive and can be used for teaching, and the separation from urban life formed by the planted framework helps give a strong sense of community.

Collegiate plans Universities composed of semi-autonomous colleges have an ancient foundation. Generally the colleges were privately funded, some, as at Oxford and Cambridge, linked to monasteries or private schools. Most formed recognisable units within the loose agglomeration of a university. The advantages of the collegiate structure are the close relationship between teacher and student, the sense of containment in physical, social and academic terms, and the well developed typology for the college unit (gatehouse, quad, lodgings, refectory, clock tower etc). The main disadvantage is the lack of central control over the colleges, with a consequent loss of identity of the university as a whole.

Colleges make successful residential units but they do not lend themselves to faculty structures. The extent of gardens or enclosed courts leads to large land take per student and high maintenance costs. In addition, the common elements of the university such as library, lecture theatres, laboratories or sports facilities, may be some way removed from the college.

Notwithstanding these disadvantages, the collegiate university remains a popular twentieth-century form in the UK (eg Churchill College, Cambridge, 1958) and in the USA (eg Stanford University in the form of the Main Quad, 1891). The collegiate structure readily adapts for student housing, teaching departments or research centres. Where external funds exist or where strong links with business or research occur, it is often a favoured solution since the benefactor's name can be given to the college. For the city centre campus the collegiate structure is not economical or appropriate in social terms.

Linear plans This type of campus, normally arranged around an internal street, takes advantage of linear compaction to create distinctive and relatively economic

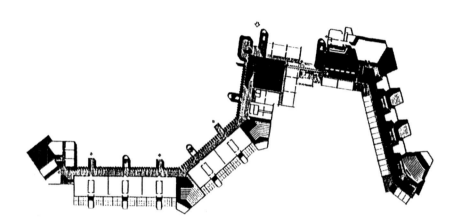

1.10 Scarborough College, Toronto, Canada (1966).

universities. The longitudinal configuration allows for growth at either end and cross axes are easily created to form sub-developments of student housing or teaching areas (eg California State University, Chico). Normally three- or four-storeys high at the centre, the linear masterplan can twist or turn to follow site contours, to respond to view or sun path, or to connect with the external infrastructure.

The internal street or mall within such development provides a useful point of contact for students and academic staff alike. In harsh climates, the sheltered walkway performs much the same function as the external street of sunnier climes. Along the mall such facilities as library, refectory, bookshop and student union offices can be conveniently located (eg Sheffield Hallam University).

The main disadvantages of the linear form are the lack of a sense of orientation within the central street, the difficulty of establishing an identity for faculties, departments or research units located in its form, and the separation of external landscape from university buildings. The economical nature of the dense linear campus has, however, led to its frequent use over the past generation (University of East Anglia, 1965, by Denys Lasdun and Partners and in British Columbia at Simon Fraser University, 1970, by Erickson and Massey).

The linear form leads to the megastructure approach to campus design. Here greater height is exploited to add even more functions within the linear shell, sometimes involving student housing at upper levels. Density within linear forms leads to remarkable efficiencies of layout due to the multiple exploitation of structure, circulation and services, but such campuses can be alienating and are often removed from the building traditions of their region. Problems of crime and security are common in this type of campus.

Grid-dominated plans This masterplan type is a natural development of the linear form. The grid, whether or not biased in favour of one of its axes, provides a rational basis for university planning. The orthogonal layout with streets, pedestrian paths or infrastructure corridors at right angles to each other exploits land well while providing a variety of routes across the campus (eg California State University, Sacramento). The permeable nature of gridded layouts suits the democratic ideals of many universities, while providing a high measure of flexibility in the use of land. Different blocks within the grid can be used for a variety of educational functions and there is usually space within the rectangular parcels of land for external growth.

Gridded masterplans have been widely adopted for campus layouts in the twentieth century. It was the form Charles A Platt adopted for the Illinois Institute of Technology in 1922, subsequently extended on the same lines by Mies van der Rohe from 1939 onwards. Gridded campus layouts are particularly common in the USA where the urban street system is readily extended onto universities and then

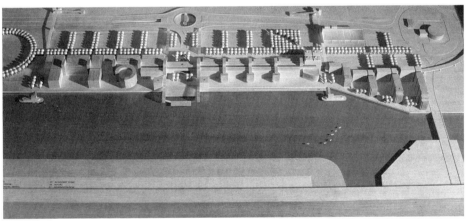

1.12 University of East London, Royal Docks Campus, London, UK. Masterplan by RMJM, detailed design by Edward Cullinan & Partners.

broken down into ever smaller units to form development parcels, then departmental buildings and finally teaching rooms. Sub-division of grids provides flexibility and internal changeability but the anonymity of structures and spaces formed can undermine the sense of academic place.

Modular-based plans This type of masterplan is composed of repeating units which, in different configurations and scales of use, provides a kit of parts for the university. It has the advantage of giving the university great visual order, and through mass production, of providing economies of scale. Often based upon prefabricated elements of construction and dimensional co-ordination, it allows for fast, relatively cheap construction. Modularity is suited to elements of the university which consist of repeatable units, such as student housing or research facilities, or to universities constructed to standardised plans.

The disadvantages of visual monotony and lack of differentiation of functional hierarchies are offset not only by cost and aesthetic consistency, but by the establishment of a clear order into which future growth can take place. Modularity is favoured by the cost conscious, and, by working with building contractors at the design stage, can lead to high standards of construction per unit of cost. Since the emphasis is upon the modularity of building, as against space, this approach to masterplanning can lead to dull and poorly considered external spaces.

Molecular-growth plans Masterplanning based upon molecular principles consists of a grouping of buildings in logical relationship according to functional, non-linear hierarchies. Each building of varying form and function is connected by roads and paths to create a network of interacting units. The molecules are the buildings, the paths are the lines of force which hold the elements in place. Each building is composed of some identical parts and some different ones thereby allowing separate internal programmes to be externally expressed.

In the molecular system space for growth is essential. Unlike the collegiate, or linear, it is external space which determines the nuance of layout not compact building mass. Hence the molecular masterplan suits a university with plenty of land to develop and a clear sense of future needs. In some ways the molecular and modular systems share

characteristics but the degree of differentiation in the molecular, the non-orthogonal groupings on site, and the avoidance of a unifying prefabricated language distinguish the molecular. In the molecular there is, however, a degree of order which grows from the use of a repertoire of forms, materials or details. The molecular is not a question of celebrating chaos but of using self-referenced spatial patterns to shape development. The molecular allows growth, agglomeration or subdivision to occur in such a fashion than the campus retains a sense of vitality and a feeling of order.

Radial plans This masterplan form adds the benefits of the gridded layout to that of place making. Normally the radial masterplan consists of a central point about which lines or clusters of campus development radiate. The pivot is often the senate house or library (as at the Webb and Bell plan for the University of Manchester, 1895) but can be an arbitrary point on the campus (eg University of Essex, 1963, by Architects' Co-Partnership).

Radial layouts provide better orientation than those planned on gridded lines, there is less a feeling of abstraction, and the arms which radiate outwards can forge subtle relationships with the wider landscape. The flow of lines in the radial plan helps create a sense in one direction of building focus and in the other of external contemplation.

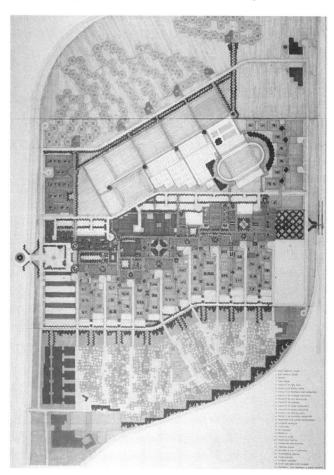

1.13 University of Helwan, Egypt. Masterplan by Skidmore, Owings and Merrill.

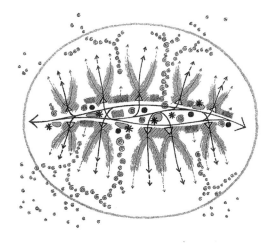

1.14 University of Bath, UK. Masterplan by RMJM.

12

The radial when combined with strongly defined axial elements creates the kind of distinctive masterplan required of many modern universities. The complexity which grows from the radial approach helps establish place specific relationships between faculty buildings, or between shared facilities (such as libraries) and more private areas (such as student housing).

Ad hoc This form of masterplan is barely a plan at all though it is a common reality of how universities develop over time. The ad hoc masterplan accepts little or no spatial pattern other than the functional demands of access and daylight, neither is there a considered relationship between building types or functional hierarchies, nor are pedestrian routes well established or articulated.

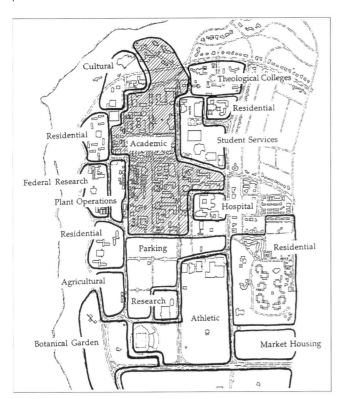

1.15 Functional land-use planning at the University of British Columbia, Vancouver, Canada. It is difficult to discern the organisational structure of this masterplan.

The ad hoc is rarely advocated as a starting point for university growth but becomes an inevitable consequence of the lack of thought by university vice-chancellors, presidents and deans. Frequently ad hoc solutions are the result of changing values over time. The original campus plan may be thought inappropriate but rather than adopt a modified plan, administrators frequently follow no plan at all. Each building development is considered on its own merits with little regard to the whole. Sometimes there are delightful accidents, a kind of happy collage of built form or intent but too frequently the ad hoc results in a damaging dislocation of campus identity, the fracturing of internal routes, and the obscuring of historic or cherished buildings. The redevelopment of Edinburgh University after 1960 could be cited as evidence of this (mostly under the influence of Basil Spence), so too can many inner-city campuses in the USA such as the University of St Louis. With both cases, intended order has been compromised by a lack of consistency in campus planning brought about by burgeoning student numbers and unclear architectural typologies.

The effect of time

University growth is marked by unpredictability which stems from the long timescale of campus evolution. Some universities today are several centuries old and even what we call 'new universities' in the UK are now in their second or third generation. Though nine categories of masterplan can be readily discerned, it is rare for a single approach to survive for much longer than a century. The modularity of the University of York has, for instance, been altered out of recognition, the clarity of the landscape-dominated plan of the University of Stirling or that of the University of California at Berkeley has been obscured by subsequent development. Similarly, McGill's pine-clad hillside campus is not a great deal more today than a memory of former ambition.

If masterplan intentions have a short life, how then are universities to proceed? The answer lies in three principles. First, it is better to have a masterplan than no plan at all. Second, the adopted plan must be flexible enough to cater for the unpredictable. Third, spatial plans need to

1.16 Landscape and building design giving order to the campus. Ohio State University, masterplan (1995), by Sasaki Associates and Michael Dennis Associates.

be supplemented by design codes (on such matters as building heights, materials, landscaping). Universities require a particular type of masterplan – one which reflects the long timescales involved, which acknowledges the presence of earlier, perhaps dated, plans and which forges a link with the evolving relationship between campus design and academic mission. The efficient utilisation of land is not a sufficient basis for development unless a university's sense of history and geography are acknowledged. The challenge of the university masterplan is to create an academic community and a learning environment which survives over time.

Unlike most developers of land, university authorities can take a long-term view of operations. Many universities today are already hundreds of years old and the bulk of Western universities can claim to be in their third or fourth generation of development. Coupled with their size and lack of fundamental change in terms of what constitutes a university, the modern campus can move over time towards greater density, complexity and richness. There is no reason why change cannot be embraced and turned to aesthetic advantage. By developing in such a fashion that the urban grain and foci are respected, subsequent buildings can enhance the overall environment by, for example, reinforcing the campus centre or by clarifying internal routes and external linkages.

The longevity of the campus provides the opportunity, if change is well managed, to create places of strong identity and environmental richness. The spirit of the original masterplan needs, however, to pervade subsequent decisions with regard to spatial arrangement, land use and building configuration. It is no good as often happens for one urban typology to be substituted for another, or for physical disarray to obscure cherished campus landmarks. The forces of change can bring richness or chaos depending upon how well the development process is managed.

The sense of historical layering is a feature of many successful older campuses. Each phase of development is expressed in a different style or method of building, and each new programme brings a fresh wave of vitality to the campus. Mature campuses such as Harvard or

1.16 Landscape and building design giving order to the campus. Ohio State University, masterplan (1995), by Sasaki Associates and Michael Dennis Associates.

London University exhibit the benefits of large-scale incremental growth managed according to enduring masterplan principles. Since most universities consist of agglomerations of large and individually-shaped build-

1.17 Academic 'place' at Stanford University, Palo Alto, USA, established in 1891 by Shepley, Rutan and Coolidge.

ings, the unity is not the result of collections of identical parts (as in housing or business estates) but of the sharing of aesthetic or spatial precepts.

It is a characteristic of universities that each building is created for a slightly different function, has specific service or access needs, and often requires a particular location. Whether it be library, sports hall, lecture theatre block or departmental building, the functional difference drives a specific response to built form. The diversity of physical objects which stems from such pressure produces campuses more marked by chaotic order than ordered chaos. Without a clear long-term plan and supporting policies on landscape, urban and building design, the chance of creating richness and character are slim. Of those universities which have survived change without destroying the sense of academic place – Oxford, Stanford and The Sorbonne for example – it has been through consistent guardianship of the urban realm.

University of Virginia, Charlottesville: the precursor of the modern American campus

The layout of the University of Virginia has had a profound effect upon the design of campuses in the USA, and arguably elsewhere. There have been two influences: the first, the establishment of the importance of a central landscaped axis through the university for social and academic discourse.

The second, the need for architectural expression in the layout of the campus in order to reflect the pedagogic ambitions of the university and its different academic disciplines. The University of Virginia (1817–26) was designed by Thomas Jefferson working in partnership with architectural advisors William Thornton and Benjamin Latrobe. The layout is simple: a wide, tree-lined avenue terminated at one end by the university library and kept open at the other to provide a prospect over the plantations. The avenue, nearly 60 metres wide and 300 metres long, was intended as a space for recreation and amenity, and for academic exchange as well as campus gossip.

The avenue was lined by the separate departments of the university each under a professor. There were ten departments facing the avenue with their own buildings – each though classical in style was to reflect in detailed architectural terms the different subjects taught. As Jefferson devised the curriculum for the university, selected the site, prepared the masterplan and supervised the construction, he was well placed to ensure that architectural and academic ambitions were in unison.

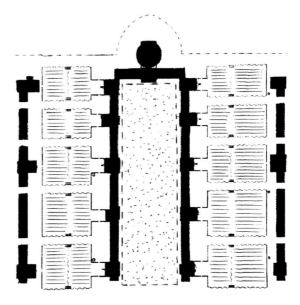

1.18 University of Virginia, Charlottesville, USA. Thomas Jefferson's plan of 1822 redrawn by author.

Jefferson was keen to demonstrate through his campus that mind and body developed together. This distinctively American ideal so characteristic of modern academic life finds expression not only in the central linear green but the arcaded routes linking the various buildings together where Jefferson said the students could exercise even in inclement weather. Behind the linking pavilions were gardens, intended originally for growing crops and as sanitation space between the 'outdoor conveniences'. The 'night soil' from the toilets was to fertilise the land, creating a biological system to complement the academic one. In this sense Jefferson's ideals came close to the current concept of 'sustainable development', especially with the students helping with crop harvesting and the professors enjoying the provision of fields on campus for grazing their cows and horses.

Jefferson's masterplan is ordered and rational. The positioning of residential quarters to the rear of the teaching pavilions where students and slaves could engage without violating regulations then in place, gave an essential propriety to the arrangement. The architectural highlight is undoubtedly the university library which was the only building in the plan allowed to introduce a circle into the composition. Designed by Jefferson himself, the rotunda-shaped reading room reflected the architect's belief in the value of the mind and as a consequence of learning to American society.

The curriculum, layout and subjects taught had a rational classical basis. There is an extraordinary unity in the elements, and, since Jefferson as the first Rector had the

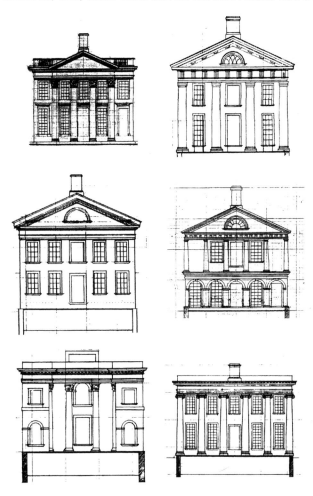

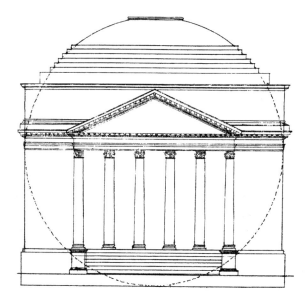

1.19 Library, University of Virginia, Charlottesville, USA, by Thomas Jefferson.

1.20 Selection of professor's houses, University of Virginia, Charlottesville, USA.

1.21 Central area of Yale University, Newport, USA. Notice the lawn between High Street and York Street with its terminating library.

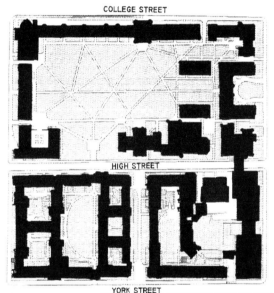

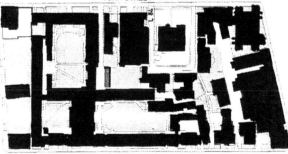

America, is not so much the intellectualising of the plan and academic system but the use of neo-Georgian buildings – themselves a mockery of his ideals.

One neglected aspect of Jefferson's much discussed plan is the thought given to future expansion. The configuration of buildings and spaces allowed for extendibility in both directions – along the axis of the avenue and to the rear into the space between teaching pavilions and dormitories. The plan is essentially a grid-iron crossed by a central linear square. The grid is the basis for many colonial plantation towns and here Jefferson adapted the form to give both academic clarity to the layout and to provide space for growth. In his report as a commissioner Jefferson explained that one of the advantages of the plan was that it admitted to 'enlargement to any degree to which the institution may extend in future times'.[2]

Stanford University, Palo Alto, California: the changing face of a university

Few universities display so well in their physical form the changing ideals of campus design than Stanford. Conceived in 1884, as a memorial to their only child who died at the age of fifteen, it was founded by Jane and Deland Stanford

1.22 Main Quad, Stanford University, Palo Alto, USA.

power to appoint, the teachers, professors and staff were of like mind. Until the construction of the University of Virginia, campuses in Europe and the Americas had grown in piecemeal fashion. At best there were pockets of order within a collage of differing academic ambitions as at Oxford. Jefferson imposed an indelible system upon higher education: one where the politics of space, the operation of the academic programme, building form and detail all subscribed to the same basic philosophy. One can trace its influence on the campuses at Berkeley, Stanford, Harvard and Yale. But none quite measures up to the rigour of the Virginia plan, although many take elements and adjust them to local conditions. Sadly, the commonest legacy of Jefferson's work, at least in as a co-educational university to help create a society of 'cultured and useful citizens'. Using gold mining and railway fortunes, the Stanfords gifted the 3,237 hectare estate on which the university sits and appointed Frederick Law Olmsted to give it shape. Although Olmsted's naturalistic masterplan was subsequently compromised by the client's preference for Beaux-Arts building groupings, the stamp of nature has never entirely been erased.

The palm-lined gardens, quads and streets of Stanford provide a picturesque backcloth for successive generations of architects. The original buildings, designed by Shepley, Rutan and Coolidge in 1891, are in the California Mission style with a clear debt also to Henry Hobson Richardson. Semi-circular Romanesque arches march around the Main Quad imposing an arcaded order upon learning. Built of finely carved yellow sandstone beneath red pantiled roofs, the image of collegiate interdisciplinarity remains powerful today. Although the original quadrangle and its secondary axes recall an Oxbridge college, Stanford placed all of its early faculties into an interconnected composition of wings, gateways and courtyards. Only the library, church and art gallery were separate structures.

The strength of the initial conception provides an indelible planning framework today. Palm Drive, the Oval and main Quad establish a landscaped axis orientated roughly north–south while Campus Drive, Serra Mall and Panama Mall form the principal cross routes along which subsequent buildings are located. Periodically secondary quads, such as Jordan Quad, define terminations and key buildings, such as Hoover Tower, sit across the axis giving a sense of orientation to the whole. The malls and quads are more than the legacy of Beaux-Arts planning: they provide the corridors for various infrastructure services from water mains to fibre optics. This has allowed new buildings, such as the Gates Computer Science Building, to sit side-by-side with the old. Over a century or more of life the Stanford campus has become more complex, denser in form, yet it has retained a sense of image and orientational legibility.

Like many large universities Stanford is best seen as a town in its own right. The key ingredients of a formal centre with loosely-shaped suburban residential and business parks reflects the development structure of many American cities. Yet it has managed to accommodate central redevelopment without disruption to the whole. This is largely because of the rational nature of the masterplan and a policy of severe car restriction in all but the peripheral areas. Such is the acknowledged success of the collaboration between Olmsted and

1.23   Green Library, Stanford University, Palo Alto, USA.

1.24   Sculpture by Auguste Rodin at Stanford University, Palo Alto, USA.

Shepley, Rutan and Coolidge that the pattern of quadrangles and connecting malls forms the basis of the new Science and Engineering complex.

The richly carved arcaded Main Quad is entered by gateways, most marked by free-standing sculpture including works by Auguste Rodin and Henry Moore. They provide points of reference and reflection en route to seminar or lecture. Public art and campus sport are important elements of the original plan, ensuring that students developed in a well rounded fashion. When the admittedly decorative original buildings were completed in 1891, and the first staff appointments were being made, the president D S Jordan wrote that 'Mr Stanford wants me to get the best [staff]. He wants no ornamental or idle professors'.[3]

Because of its premier position in the sciences (there are currently fourteen Nobel Laureates among the academic community) Stanford helped lead the growth of high-tech industries in the US. The creation in 1951 of the Stanford Research Park, linked to the School of Engineering, provided an important early bridge between research scholars and the business community. Of the 160 companies located on the Park today some, such as Sun Microsystems and Hewlett-Packard, were started by faculty members. Five years later in 1955 the Stanford Shopping Center was opened, a 28-hectare retail development whose profits, along with the Science Park, fund student scholarships. With the size of its graduate student community exceeding that of undergraduate, research scholarships and the science infrastructure are particularly important to Stanford.

Growth of the Science Park, Shopping Center, the Medical Center and various student villages has been by exploiting the lands at (or beyond) the edge of the campus rather than redevelopment nearer to the centre. This has had the effect of protecting the character of the original conception and providing points of growth where they can be serviced by car. Even in the centre, the limited redevelopment has respected the spatial parameters laid down in 1891, and some recent buildings such as the Gates Computer Science Building by the architect Robert Stern, echo Stanford's arcaded tradition.

With fifteen thousand students and over five thousand academic staff at Stanford, movement of people on campus is mainly via a free bus service, on foot or

1.25 William Gates Computer Science Building, Stanford University, Palo Alto, USA, by Robert Stern.

bicycle. Private cars are banned from the core of the campus which is organised around a series of one-way traffic loops. Many journeys between buildings for service deliveries are made by electric vehicles. With its contribution of over $1 billion to the regional economy of Northern California, its own parks, water mains, 49-megawatt power station and hospital, Stanford prides itself upon being a self-sustaining community – a model of sustainability applied to higher education.[4]

French Origins: an alternative tradition

In contrast to Oxford or Cambridge and American campuses, the older colleges which make up the ancient uni-

1.26 Faculty of Medicine, University of Paris (1770), France.

versity area of the Sorbonne in Paris are not collegiate in the sense of quadrangles and gateways, but urban buildings placed side-by-side along narrow streets. Although there are small squares and locked entrances and gardens, the character of the university quarter of Paris is one of urban agglomeration of buildings of some substance. Each part of the university is not today a college but a faculty with the emphasis not upon student residences but teaching and laboratory space. Since each faculty also has its own library, dining room and main lecture theatre, the ancient universities of Paris are closer to the contemporary arrangement than the more domestic buildings of Oxford and Cambridge.

Paris along with Bologna boast the oldest universities in Europe, and although monastic and collegiate in origin, the present buildings around the Sorbonne date mainly from the sixteenth to eighteenth centuries. Typical is the Collège de France (1610) with its fine portico marking the entrance set behind a small courtyard enclosed by railings. There is an openness of character and order of layout which helps signal the spread of humanism which was the basis for the college. Teaching was from the outset free and open to the public with a statue of the benefactor Guillaume Budé beckoning to visitors. A similar arrangement exists at the Faculty of Medicine (1770) which has a screen wall to the street, not solid but open with railings and relatively friendly entrances. A statue to the anatomist Bichat stands in the courtyard facing the public street with its back to the lecture hall. Inside there is a faculty library with 650,000 books, a museum of medicine and rooms for professors. This too was designed as a civic building as opposed to a college with gestures towards public enlightenment, not private education.

To walk through the old university quarter of Paris is to experience the full potential of architecture to express the values of higher education. Classicism prevails as the adopted style but it is the geometry of forms and the rational nature of space which endures. Streets exist to link together informal promenades of college buildings. Squares where they occur, as around the Panthéon, house the shared facilities – church, Bibliothèque Ste-Geneviève

and the main law library for Paris – all arranged in formal splendour.

Typical of the contrast in Paris between collegiate architecture and public ensemble are the historic Ecole des Beaux-Arts and Ecole Polytechnique. Each is loosely arranged around courtyards or streets but the sense of organic growth generally asserts greater presence than harsh geometric order. In them too it is possible to read the location of library, studio, lecture theatre and science laboratory from the forms employed. In this sense these buildings have more useful lessons for the modern university than the more ordered and domestic colleges of Oxford or Cambridge.

Cape Town University: the colonial legacy

Typical of a university with a well ordered plan is the University of Cape Town in South Africa. Founded in 1829, the university moved to its present site on the slopes of Table Mountain in 1918. With an endowment by Cecil Rhodes of the Groote Schuur estate and a significant private donation for faculty buildings, the university appointed the architect Sir Herbert Baker on Rhodes' recommendation to prepare the masterplan. The plan is remarkable in two respects: first, it was conceived as a series of curving streets, anchored by a central library, which stepped gracefully down the mountainside to overlook the sports fields. Second, Baker had the sense

1.27 Street-based campus planning. University of Cape Town, South Africa.

to anticipate growth using the unterminated ends of wide curving streets as the vehicle for future campus expansion. The curved nature of the streets achieved the further benefits of allowing the new university to meld with the contours of a wonderful mountainside site as well as embracing the concept of sporting excellence.

A powerful cross axis occurs at the mid point and is aligned on the peak of Table Mountain. This axis which consists mainly of grand steps in the Edwardian manner is itself terminated by the congregation hall (Jameson Hall) used for ceremonial purposes. The role of the hall is both symbolic – it is here that students parade on graduation in their gowns – and visual, commanding a view across the rugby fields perched on the lower slopes to the cricket pitch beyond. The curving streets and the cross axis bring the hall into visibility from every part of the campus, including the playing fields.

Baker was skilful in his positioning of the parts. The Jagger Library sat alongside Jameson Hall with the Student Union building on the opposite side of the square. Hence, library, union and hall are related in a grand gesture of learning. At the time of writing the library is being extended to form a U-shaped embrace around the hall, making a direct link via a computer-based learning centre to the student union. Another clever arrangement by Baker and his assistant J M Soloman is the way in which the slope of the mountainside brings the sports field into close contact with the heart of the campus. The lowest of the three main streets acts as a promenade set high above the rugby pitches. As a consequence the top side of the campus faces onto the pine-clad mountainside and the lower side onto the sports pitches. This, with the ever present Jameson Hall, gives a campus of twenty thousand students remarkable legibility.

The research facilities exist as perimeter forming relatively autonomous compounds around the edge of the campus. The Medical School is a large version of one of these (as it is at Stanford) with its own access road set on the same contours some way to the west. The student village where many undergraduates stay is located lower down the slope on the approximate axis of Jameson Hall. Whereas the upper campus looks across a terrace of rugby fields, the lower campus revolves around the cricket ground. As in many

1.27 Street-based campus planning. University of Cape Town, South Africa.

South African campuses, sport plays an important role in establishing geometric order for the whole campus.

The single lesson of the University of Cape Town campus is the need for a coherent plan at the outset. Baker could not anticipate all the changes but he provided a framework whereby it could take place in an orderly fashion. When the Groote Schuur estate was first developed by the university there were only six hundred students, yet a thirty-fold increase in numbers and educational complexity has occurred without loss of spatial integrity. Of all the African campuses, the University of Cape Town has the greatest correspondence between an educational ideal and the spatial integration of buildings, landscape and sport. However one sad result of the endeavour was that Soloman committed suicide when he discovered that he could not realise the fine detail of his architectural ambition due to rising costs.

Notes

1. Richard P Dober, *Campus Architecture: Buildings in Groves of Academe*, McGraw-Hill (1996), New York, p 230.
2. James B Conant, *Thomas Jefferson and the Development of American Public Education*, University of California Press (1962), Berkeley, p 14.
3. Details on Stanford University are gleaned from *Stanford Facts* (1998), edited by Shelley Hébert, and the Stanford Web site at www.stanford.edu/.
4. Ibid.

CHAPTER 2

Masterplans or development frameworks

In the development of the campus there are clear differences between the use of masterplans and development frameworks. The former are spatial, three-dimensional and visual; the latter deal with codes, standards and heights but are usually two-dimensional and abstract. The advantage of masterplans is that one obtains a sense of aesthetic qualities as well as the representation of the practical and functional solutions to campus growth. The development framework on the other hand is more of a design guide which prescribes in general terms the

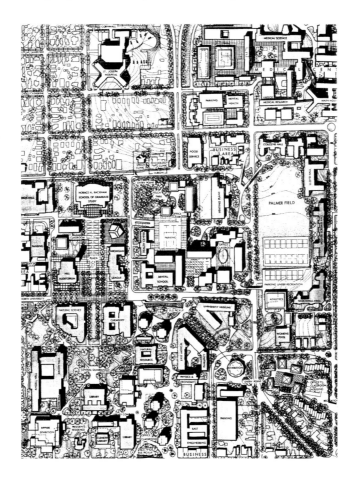

2.1 Formal masterplan, University of Michigan, Ann Arbor, USA, prepared by Johnson, Johnson and Roy, landscape architects.

2.2 Development framework, University of British Columbia, Vancouver, Canada.

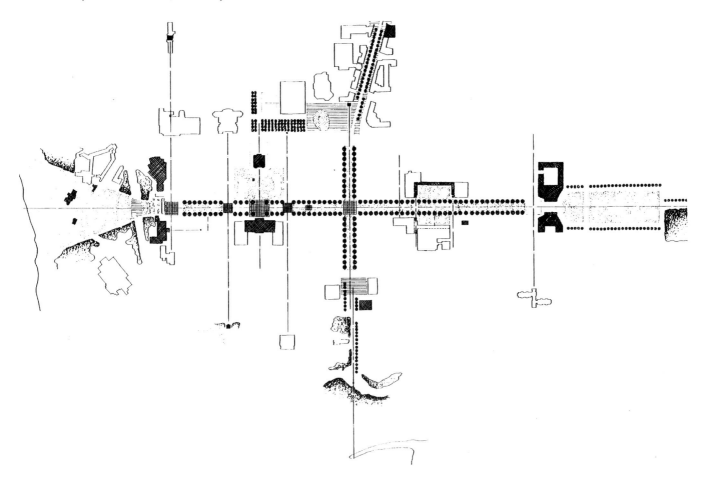

preferred form for new buildings, planting, roads and other infrastructure provision. Generally speaking, formal master-plans are more common in the USA than in Europe, giving American campuses an order and consistency often lacking in their cities.

Potential developers, such as research partners and private institutions, can obtain through the masterplan a picture of what they may be willing to buy or at least support. Image is important in generating enthusiasm for a new building, especially when partnership funding is involved (such as the Public Finance Initiative – PFI). Image too may help with securing planning permission and in the attraction of new students and staff. However, the

formal and visual image may become an impediment to campus growth when the assumptions upon which the masterplan was based change. No matter how attractively structured and designed, a campus plan out of step with changing priorities will not help secure investment. This is why periodic review, usually every five years, is needed.

Development frameworks on the other hand are more flexible in format and can serve the objectives of securing ordered growth and attracting inward invest-ment more effectively than the traditional masterplan. One may not obtain a sense of how things will look but there will be a rational structure behind how and where new

2.3   Campus perspective, Ohio State University, Columbus, Ohio. Caudill Rowlett and Scott (1962).

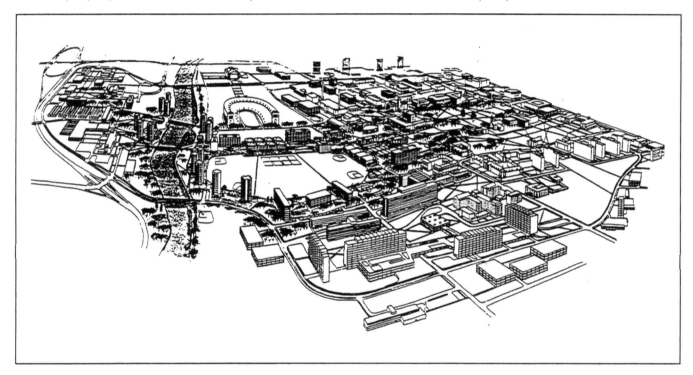

faculty buildings occur. Typical of the development framework is a campus plan with shadows cast giving some indication of the relative height of buildings, plus a number of supporting design codes covering such matters as sight-lines, street corner definition, arcades to shelter pedestrian movement, skyline punctuation, materials and so forth. Besides buildings, the development framework will also prescribe standards and policies for car parking, tree planting and infrastructure provision below ground.

Whereas the masterplan is likely to be supported by the architectural perspective, the framework leaves such matters to the designers of the individual buildings. Since campus growth occurs over generations, often involving many different architects, the benefit of aesthetic flexibility is obvious. However, the development framework can become so abstract that it fails to fire anybody's imagination, and without vision there can be a lack of inward investment.

The answer at larger universities is to combine the benefits of both development frameworks and masterplans by using the latter as an inset in the former. A campus-wide development framework can be supported by formal masterplans for specific areas, such as the academic centre, a student housing village, research park, etc. As the need arises a masterplan can be prepared for growth pockets or those areas where pressure perennially occurs. By having a hierarchy of plans, each more specific as the focus is turned upon particular sites, the benefits of flexibility and architectural order can be combined.

At smaller universities a single masterplan may suffice. Order is needed to ensure that physical development reflects the mission of the university. The spatial pattern of buildings should mirror the pedagogic ideals of the institution – in this the masterplan is a vital tool in guiding campus building towards a common aim across generations. For the inner city campus the masterplan is often put under pressure due to changing external conditions around the

university. The greenfield campus can generally rely upon an unchanging physical context but this is not true of universities in urban locations. As a consequence, the type of masterplan is not fixed but needs to respond to the environment in which the university finds itself. The web of pedestrian connectivity, for instance in the inner city, is more complex and important than for a university surrounded by agricultural land, yet in the countryside the landscape framework of the university may be of greater concern than for the urban campus. The masterplan needs to reflect in content and style these variations.

The masterplan and development framework both identify sites for new buildings and give potential funders (Higher Education Funding Council for England – HEFCE, Lottery, private benefactors) a clear context of what is proposed. Since much university development is the result of joint ventures and private funding initiatives, the scale, footprint, height and general appearance of the prospective building is important in securing confidence in the project. Evidence suggests that those universities with a clearer sense of their physical as well as academic development are more successful in attracting inward investment. Hence, the masterplan is not just a space organising document, it is equally the means of promoting a university and attracting funds.

Since universities are large, land and resource hungry, self-governing organisations their masterplans or development frameworks need to correspond with the ambitions of the local authority in which they are located. The campus plan and that of the city council should synchronise. Without a physical plan on behalf of the university, it is difficult for both parties to ensure that matters in which they have a common interest, such as public transport, housing provision, recreation and policing, are tackled in a co-ordinated fashion. Hence a further advantage of the campus masterplan is that it can assist the local authority in deciding upon land-use or transportation priorities in support of the university's own ambitions. Without a well developed masterplan it is difficult for the town council or state planning department to ensure a common framework for the rationalisation of land at the perimeter of the campus. Where the two are not

developed in parallel there can be missed opportunities for the development of business parks or student villages. So the campus masterplan needs to identify land for growth or rationalisation within the estate of the university as well as connections and expansion outside the campus.

Two Case Studies of Formal Masterplans

(a)   Temasek Polytechnic, Singapore

Occupying a 30-hectare site between Tampines New Town and Bedok Reservoir, the design by Michael Wilford and Partners (1995) creates a campus for 11,500 students and 1,500 academic and support staff. The campus establishes a central focus in the form of a horseshoe-shaped administrative building with wings for separate faculties radiating from its core. There is a central plaza, open and public, which faces the town with a high level pedestrian bridge across the dual carriageway. Located to one side of

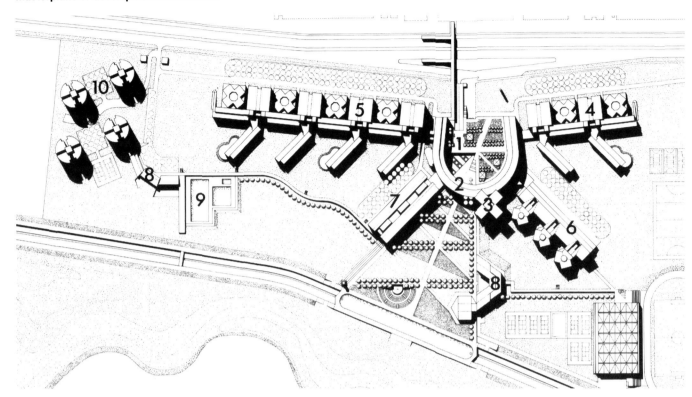

2.5 Temasek Polytechnic, Singapore, by Michael Wilford and Partners. Key: 1 Central Plaza, 2 Administration, 3 Library, 4 Applied Sciences, 5 Technology, 6 Business, 7 Design, 8 Faculty Club, 9 Sport, 10 Residences.

the horseshoe is the library which rises above all the other structures, identifying the university in the landscape and signalling the importance of book-based learning to university life.

The design is based upon the concept of a 'city of learning' with a deliberate attempt to create a megastructure of physically linked parts. Each wing is dedicated to a particular faculty – Applied Sciences, Business, Design, Technology – with the form and layout of each reflecting specific functional demands. As such the Business wing consists mainly of lecture theatres and seminar rooms, the Design school has large studios and 'crit' areas, the Technology wing has extensive workshops, and Applied Sciences has a combination of laboratories and lecture theatres.

The central administrative block contains a perimeter walkway which leads directly into the pedestrian routes which access the separate faculty buildings. Legibility and hierarchy are established by means of building design, planting, layout and the definition of types of routes. Like any city, urban design plays a key part in establishing order. For example, views of the reservoir are brought into play by cutting huge visibility slots in the wall of the horseshoe block. The prospect over water provides a sense of orientation from every part of the campus, and contrasts with both internal views within planted courts and distant views in the opposite direction over the town.

The Wilford masterplan seeks to make a landmark out of the development of the polytechnic. Compact, sculpted architecture, not pavilions in a park, is the guiding concept, with a single design practice preparing the overall plan and providing most of the buildings. There is, therefore, consistency in almost every part – both the whole and the details subscribe to the same monumental rigour. Since the university is not large, this creates a civilising, unifying environment of higher learning rather than a massive, soulless megastructure of building.

The central plaza, promenade and separate concourses for each faculty provide a form of armature which disciplines pedestrian movement. All facilities – academic, leisure, administrative and sporting – are within five minutes walk of the centre. Routes are mainly covered ways or designed as planted pergolas through campus parkland. Generally the pedestrian walkways are on the northern side of buildings in order to provide shade. A perimeter campus road system provides an unobtrusive circuit for vehicles with spurs into each node of development.

Local climate constraints and environmental conditions required inside each building influence the orientation, scale and position of buildings. For example, the lecture theatres are used to shade the studios of the design faculty building and in the engineering school staff offices protect the laboratories from excessive solar gain. The various buildings – teaching and administrative – are shallow in plan to allow breezes to flow across the depth of the building. Natural light and ventilation determine orientation of the wings as well as room depths. For instance, the narrow science block laboratories are angled so that the wind over the reservoir is channelled into the interior. A similar ploy is followed in the angling of wings between the central plaza block and the water's edge. Fresh breezes here are not only deflected to the horseshoe-shaped block but the large 'window' cut into the perimeter wall allows the breezes to reach the planted plaza centre.

The development of Temasek Polytechnic cleverly balances the need for an administrative and architectural focus with the demand also for expandability. Each wing can extend outwards as demand increases and the same logic applies to the horseshoe-shaped central block. Since the faculty buildings have their own pattern of lecture theatres, teaching space, laboratories and offices, there is a template which can readily be expanded. Temasek has refined a repertoire of different kinds of teaching environment for each faculty, thereby giving the campus academic distinctiveness. There is, therefore, a combination of consistency and specificness to faculty needs; monumentality plus rational order.

2.6 Central Plaza, Temasek Polytechnic, Singapore, by Michael Wilford and Partners.

Development	Architect	Special Features	Cost
Masterplan, Temasek Polytechnic, Singapore	Michael Wilford and Partners	• Compact, sculptural composition • Radiating plan • Extendable without loss of character • Each faculty wing has distinct quality	Not available

(b) *Dammam Campus Masterplan, King Faisal University, Saudi Arabia*

King Faisal University is divided into two campuses: one at Al Hasa and the other on the coast at Dammam. In 1977 the Saudi authorities appointed a French construction group including the architects Andrault and Parat to prepare the masterplan for the new Dammam campus. Besides an academic community the site was also to house a teaching hospital and mosque for use by the local community.

The site is a large 500-hectare estate alongside the coast road between Dammam and Al Khobar.

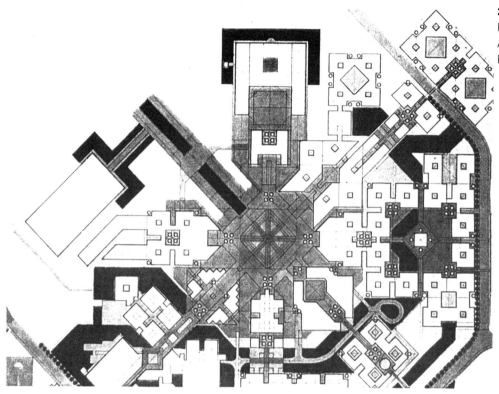

2.7 Masterplan (detail), King Faisal University, Dammam, Saudi Arabia, by Andrault and Parat with Beeah Architects.

2.8a Centre of campus, King Faisal University, Dammam, Saudi Arabia.

2.8b View of Mosque.

Being a seafront campus the perception of the water-front is a key aspect of the masterplan, and views to the sea skilfully balance the Islamic urban tradition of the internal courtyard.

The site is flat and in response Andrault and Parat designed low-lying buildings punctuated by towers. A base course of building three-and four-storeys high covers the site, counterbalanced by stair towers which project from the main facades, and periodically by the slender modern minarets of the campus mosques. A central grand mosque and associated Islamic centre orders both the plan and skyline. Designed in detail by the Saudi practice of Beeah Architects, the building generates a series of square and diagonal routes across the campus which radiate about a main central courtyard. Physically, the

28

Development	Architect	Special Features	Cost
Masterplan, Dammam Campus, King Faisal University, Saudi Arabia	Andrault and Parat with Beeah Architects	• Seaside campus with ocean views via central axis • Mosque dominates plan and arranges teaching buildings oncross axes • Islamic urban traditions blended with international design methodologies • Bio-climatic design using traditional features • Pedestrian only campus with cars kept at periphery • Use of self-contained courtyard buildings to provide phased construction	$920/m^2 in 1983, currently around $2,000/m^2

main square leads to a counter balanced composition of medical college and library in one direction, and mosque and open seafront in the other. It is an arrangement which conceptually joins the land with the sea, learning with religion, and health with knowledge.

The other faculty and teaching buildings are located in the angles between the main buildings. They share a minor alignment being placed at 45 degrees to the main composition. Outside this central grouping is placed an orbital road system which leads in turn to the student village, sports facilities and research laboratories. These elements share the same geometry as the centre but at lower densities and near the waterfront the irregular outline of the coastline moderates the orthogonal layout.

The Islamic logic of urban site planning based upon right-angled and diagonal grids is balanced to the south of the campus by a linear axis of teaching and research facilities. Here each school shares a central palm planted courtyard and fountain which links via another axis to community facilities such as playing fields at one end, and the computer centre and conference hall at the other. A further perimeter road system handles parking (there is 100 per cent staff and student provision at the university) and joins the Dammam campus to the public highway. A perimeter circuit of dual carriageways allows the campus centre to be retained for pedestrians who walk the 300 metres from the nearest parking area.

The layout and design of individual buildings brings the best of Western rational architecture and Islamic tradition together. Building in heavyweight concrete and stone with narrow windows moderates the desert temperature, as does the combination of narrow and wider courtyards. Water too plays a key part. It is used in courtyards to cool the air and is employed via larger lakes and canals to irrigate the wider landscape. Added to this, pedestrian routes are shaded by building overhangs, and, being placed on pilotis, the faculty buildings benefit from cooling of the soffits by air currents drawn across water.

The architectural character of the campus is the most Islamic of any recent university in the Middle East. The banning of cars from all but the perimeter, the use of an austere, little decorated and almost windowless architectural vocabulary, the clear sense of hierarchy in the provision of buildings and configuration of routes, the employment throughout of interconnected courtyards, and the dominating presence of the central mosque give this large new campus relevance to cultures which wish to maintain their identity in the face of globalising education.

Two Case Studies of Development Frameworks

(a)   West Campus, Cambridge University, UK

In 1997 Cambridge University broke with tradition and prepared plans for a major new science and research campus 8 kilometres to the west of the city. Occupying a site of 66 hectares, the development framework was prepared by MacCormac Jamieson Prichard to give structure to development over a thirty-year period. Besides teaching and research, the site will also accommodate sports and social facilities, student residences and a park-and-cycle system.

The aim is to create a largely self-contained new science campus which promotes interaction between researchers, and between the academic and commercial research community. Inevitably, the mas-

terplan strikes a balance between spatial order in the layout of buildings and future flexibility. The evolving needs of research and the changing aspirations of what constitutes an academic community are finely balanced in the plan. With a thirty-year time horizon it is clear that different architects will be involved in design and since technology and taste will alter as much as academic philosophy, the emphasis in the plan is upon principle – both academic and urban design. Of the first is a commitment to social and intellectual interaction through the provision of pedestrian routes, squares and enclosed college-type gardens. Of the second is a concern for phasing of development so

2.9   Development Framework for the West Cambridge site, University of Cambridge, UK, by MacCormac, Jamieson and Prichard.

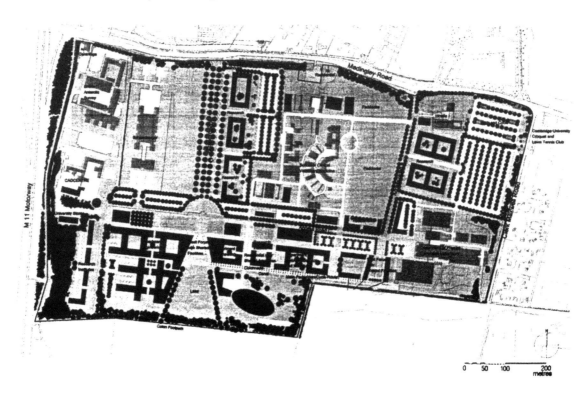

that visual cohesion is provided initially as well as in the longer term. There is also a balance of landscape and building design, and a concern to ensure that site ecology is not sacrificed by excessive use of hard man-made materials.

The infrastructure of roads, services and buildings complements the aspiration towards place making. This is evident in the geometric pattern which never quite dominates the natural order of landscape and ecology around and within the proposed campus. Being alongside the M11 motorway there is a thick bank of woodland planting which absorbs cycle and walkways to the west, while lakes and rivers do the same to the south. Within this natural system a series of courtyard research buildings are planned, most with central gardens or atria, contrasting with linear buildings for teaching. A separate student village is planned and sports facilities will provide landmarks around the campus edge. A unifying avenue of trees, aligned

north–south helps structure the centre of the new campus and provides sites for the major buildings.

(b) Lincoln Campus, The University of Lincolnshire and Humberside, UK

Designed by RMJM on a 16-hectare site close to the centre of historic Lincoln, this was, in 1995, the UK's first totally new university for thirty years. The site is flat, alongside a river and marina, bisected by an elevated dual carriageway, and edged to the south by a railway line. The approach is essentially linear following the line of the river with buildings and spaces facing northways towards the cathedral about 1 kilometre away. Buildings are generally narrow in plan, to maximise natural light and ventilation, and long to take advantage of fast-track construction methods. The main teaching and administrative buildings, including a learning resource centre, adopt clear span floor plates serviced from plant riser towers. The avoidance of columns and the use of major and minor planning grids gives functional flexibility while providing a strong visual order to the various buildings.

Within the logic of column-free spaces and clearly articulated service zones (including steel-cored elements for lateral stability) exists a complementary discipline of low-energy design. The intensively used areas such as lecture theatres and IT laboratories have chilled beam/displacement ventilation, elsewhere ventilation is natural with mechanical back-up in 'hot' spots. The large open-plan spaces exploit the stack effect for cooling and smoke extraction. Facades are differently treated to alleviate solar gains, noise from the adjoining railway line, and to give articulation to 'served' and 'servant' spaces.

The student village to the west consists of six clusters of accommodation blocks, each three- or four-storeys high, grouped around internal courtyards. Most study bedrooms have ensuite bathrooms and share communal kitchens. They are designed to

Development	Architect	Special Features	Cost
Science Campus, Cambridge University	MacCormac, Jamieson, Prichard	• Plan which promotes interaction between research and teaching	Not available
		• Spatial order, connectivity and hierarchy in the layout of buildings and landscape	
		• Compact centre with informal edges for student housing and sport	
		• Water as amenity and wildlife refuge	

2.10   Masterplan model, Lincolnshire and Humberside University, UK, Lincoln Campus by RMJM.

cater for student-centred IT learning and to exploit the tourist market out of term time. Although RMJM prepared the development framework and have acted as architect for the main teaching buildings, the student village was designed by a local practice, giving the overall development some variety in the detail of buildings.

The concept adopted by the University of Lincolnshire and Humberside has undeniable logic: the teaching space is so flexible it could be used as lettable office space should the university fail to attract sufficient students. The discipline of adaptability and the logic of construction, especially the structural grid of 13.5 x 7.5 metres, allows for almost unlimited functional change without incurring a cost penalty. Yet, there is a tension between place and method – between the need to create a distinctive, geographically specific centre for learning and the discipline of flexibility. This is a generic solution and one which is essentially

rational and abstract. Some may prefer a closer correspondence with the character of historic Lincoln or the language of the traditional college, but this development with its dialogue between structural

Development	Architect	Special Features	Cost
Lincoln Campus, Lincolnshire and Humberside University	RMJM	• Rational and Flexible • Floor plates dictated by building system efficiency • Articulation of landmark and background buildings. • Exploitation of water-edge for pedestrian movement	Not available

rationality, functional flexibility and environmental design, has relevance to campus development world-wide.

A similar approach was taken in 1997 by the same architects for the Coach Lane Campus at the University of Northumbria in Newcastle. Here a concrete structural frame on a 15-metre grid, exposed for thermal benefit, provides for a combination of flexibility of use, low cost, and reduced energy consumption. The design is generic with a spine of open teaching space periodically divided by service cores, circulation routes and ventilating towers. As with the development at Lincoln, the university masterplan uses long blocks of narrow plan buildings to create lines of teaching space arranged around small planted courtyards. The more specific buildings, such as library and lecture theatres, offer relief from the order and provide landmarks to aid orientation across the campus. They are also self-contained buildings so that they can be commissioned and built separately, giving variety in detailed architectural treatment.

CHAPTER 3

Picturesque enclosure versus rational planning

The changing priorities of the twentieth-century campus

The twentieth-century campus can be seen as a battle between picturesque place making and the provision of rationally designed buildings. At the turn of the century a sense of place was considered an essential component of university life; by the mid-century the emergence of functionalism gave supremacy to the building and its programme; by the end of the twentieth century a sense of place was again on the urban design agenda. There are two main reasons for the oscillations in taste: first, the relative power of vice-chancellors as opposed to architects, and second, the recognition that universities have ways of life quite distinct from the practices of the commercial world.

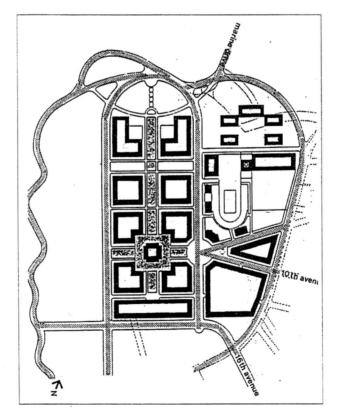

3.1 Sharpe and Thompson's masterplan of 1914 for the University of British Columbia, Vancouver, Canada. The congregation hall is in the centre. Formal campus planning based upon the Virginia model.

3.2 (Below) Joseph Bradford masterplan of 1919 for Ohio State University, Columbus, USA. A good example of the American tradition of formal campus planning.

3.3 (Right) Landscape design is the basis for most early twentieth-century campuses. Ohio State University, Columbus, Ohio. Sketch from 1995 masterplan modifications by Sasaki Associates and Michael Dennis Associates.

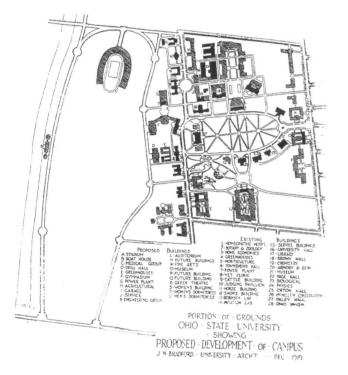

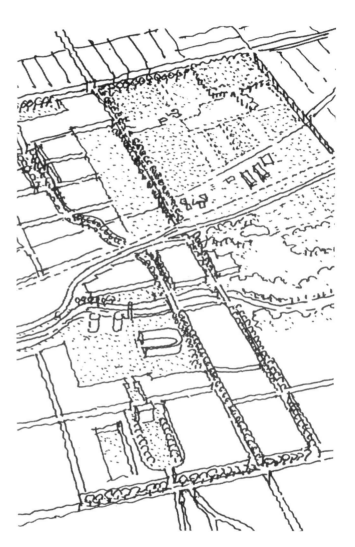

The balance of influence of taste has swung enormously. At the turn of the twentieth century, the American or British university was a bastion of exclusivity entered into either by class (or more correctly wealth) or more rarely intellect. This was expressed not only in the creation of a closed inward-looking world of quads, cloisters, dining rooms and halls of residence, but in the restriction on access imposed on others. Typically, the university of 1900 was a gated and controlled private world revolving around collegiate emblems – lawn, quadrangle, chapel, dining room and library. For the community of scholars, rectors and benefactors, this was an idealised enclave dedicated to the disciplines of higher learning.

By 1930 all this had changed. The democratising of higher education added to the new functional demands of science teaching led to more open campuses. Buildings became objects in free space, not enclosing rectangles of privileged space. The new science laboratories and teaching rooms were driven by the rigours of functionalism. Building forms flowed inevitably from the disciplines of programme, themselves shaped by the new discoveries in science, economics and business. The typical inter-war campus had a few neo-classical central buildings (library, congregation hall) surrounded by highly functional laboratories, lecture theatres and halls of residence. Picturesque enclosure was reserved, as at London and Nottingham Universities, for the centre where the images of collegiate interchange could be captured on camera. Away from the centre all was rational and shaped by the new technological order, with buildings arranged in parallel groupings around service roads. By the late 1930s the college green was a token whose echo was sounded by nostalgic vice-chancellors rather than progressive architects.

After the war functionalism grew as the new order replaced the old system. By the time of the massive expansion in higher education in the UK and elsewhere in the late 1950s and 1960s, buildings and campuses based upon a rational structure of roads, construction systems and internal programmes became the norm. Only a few architects resisted the relentless march of progress. Basil Spence at Sussex University and Paul Rudolph at Yale moderated functionalism by a sense of place making. When, in 1959, Spence was commissioned to plan the new Sussex University in rolling countryside outside Brighton, he recommended that the new buildings should not be higher than the canopy of the ancient oak trees on the site. He placed his buildings between the best tree groups, adopted a concrete column and arch palette to respond to the tectonic structure of tree trunks and branches, and used local red brick for walls and steps to blend with the building traditions of this part of England. Rudolph too added East Coast picturesque touches to his buildings, finding the expression of building services a useful excuse for monumental flourishes. Neither architect approached the task of designing buildings from a purely functional perspective.

History teaches that rationalism is a limited basis for the physical development of a university. Although a university may be rational and ordered in the development of teaching programmes, and in the management of the institution, rationality alone does not create a sense of place which is the essence of a university. There is an implicit compact in higher education which transcends the necessary functionalism of teaching, research and administration. To be truly a university there is a contract with learning (as against teaching), with a sense of a community of scholars, and with an expression through building of higher academic ideals. A university is first and foremost an ensemble of buildings dedicated to something more than the functional delivery of education. It is a place, identifiable as such through built fabric and urban space, which express these higher aspirations. Given this view the university is more than a collection of functionally rational buildings – it is essentially space where like-minded people gather in pursuit of intellectual enrichment. Viewed in this way, the university is first and foremost a 'place' where enclosure of the intellectual realm has dominance over free-flowing space. After all the rationalism and functionalism of the latter half of the twentieth century, many universities are entering the next millennium in pursuit of place, just as they did a hundred years before.

So today the building of a collegiate spirit via campus architecture is seen as important as the provision of efficient functional buildings. The relationship between learning and teaching is similar to that between architecture and building. And with the importance of architecture goes a concern for image (and hence self promotion) and an interest in intellectual as well as public space. The medium of learning is partly the medium of architecture – both rely upon space and time as the basis for reflection. Both too depend upon a distinction being drawn between public

3.4   Basil Spence with the Vice-Chancellor of Sussex University in 1959 overseeing the construction of the new university.

and private values – between the college square and private study bedroom in the case of architecture, and between the exchange of ideas and deep private thought in the case of the scholar. The university which neglects the needs of contained public space on campus will be as disadvantaged as the one which fails to distinguish between the priorities of teaching and learning.

The British campus in the twentieth century: the struggle for identity

The British campus of the twentieth century expresses particularly vividly the struggle between place making and the expression of rational, technologically pure architecture. As a pair of divergent theoretical paths the search for identity found vivid expression in the 1930s where, at London University around Bloomsbury and at Nottingham University in an Arcadian setting, the rational and picturesque stood side-by-side. The architecture of pretty enclosure and articulated facade was preferred by vice-chancellors: that of smooth surface, functional forms and horizontality by architects, engineers and progressive professors. By the time of the second growth period in universities after the war, the two paths had developed quite clear positions supported by their own schools of architects.

Basil Spence, creator of Sussex University and masterplanner for expansions of many others (Southampton, Edinburgh, Newcastle), led the reaction against a technology driven solution to campus design. Spence, at Sussex, and Denys Lasdun at the University of East Anglia, Norwich, favoured buildings which complemented rather than dominated the landscape, which used local forms or materials as a starting point for campus design, and which fused social purpose with high architectural ambition. At Sussex as mentioned earlier, Spence responded to the well wooded site outside Brighton by using local materials, dressing the whole composition in quasi-modern monastic manner. The buildings were kept to four storeys, below the height of the tree canopy, and hugged the ground in sweeping terraces and quadrangles. The style was far from timid, yet although severely contemporary for its time (the first buildings were

completed in 1961) Sussex was seen by contemporary critics as also anchored to the traditions of the Sussex countryside.

Meanwhile at the University of East Anglia (1964), Lasdun created an irregular spine of teaching buildings and laboratories from which sprouted wings of stepped halls of residence. The latter formed a great picturesque skirt around the main campus allowing the new buildings to sit happily in the Norfolk landscape. The new structures did not intrude physically upon the marsh, lakes and woodland of the site but kept themselves back so that nature could be viewed from the picture windows of dormitories or the terraces by lecture theatres. Lasdun wanted a group of university buildings which would grow like an organism uniting 'buildings and landscape … in a total vision … visually as well as functionally'.[1] But it was the Vice-Chancellor Frank Thistlethwaite who instructed the architect to provide 'a sense of place' before bowing to the pressures of growth. Flexibility in provision and the incorporation of modern construction technologies, he said, should be subserviant to the need for identity.

Lasdun's East Anglia campus was described at the same time as 'great ships floating on a sea of green'.[2] The ships were in fact promenades of learning variously angled to respond to subtleties of site and stepped so that they formed a satisfactory union with the ground. In detail the buildings are of smooth pre-cast concrete or exposed aggregate blockwork with paving in blue brick. Windows are in long horizontal

3.6 Integration of buildings and landscape design at University of East Anglia, Norwich, UK, by Denys Lasdun and Partners.

3.7 University of York, UK, by RMJM (1965).

bands or great storey-high squares. If the architecture is severe and cubic, the sense of landscape penetrates into the heart of the campus and from many rooms, most particularly student residences, there are uninterrupted panoramas across rolling countryside. In detail East Anglia is more stark than Sussex, the surfaces are minimal with texture not colour providing relief. Lasdun's buildings at the University of East Anglia have been described as the best Brutalist architecture of its time in the UK, but the sculptural tendencies are always striving to give a sense of place. East Anglia cannot be described as nowhere architecture, this is a campus which forms an identifiable union with place. The ziggurat-shaped student residences may suffer solar gain in the summer or excessive heat loss in the winter, but they are one of the great architectural experiments of their age.

In contrast to these place-making campuses of the early 1960s Britain embarked upon the construction of a number of more rationally designed new universities. Several employ system building techniques (such as York University with the adoption of CLASP prefabrication) which put the needs of rational technology before picturesque enclosure or landscape definition. At York, designed in 1962 by RMJM, the use of the college faculty system was not matched by any change in architectural order. Every college was subject to the discipline of CLASP, the metal-frame and concrete system, which provided the structural, spatial and material logic throughout. The single unifying element which unites the

architecture is a lake covering 6 hectares at the centre of the campus.

The academic and social ideals at York reflect directly the programme for the new universities at the time. Besides the college system, there was emphasis placed upon the tutorial and seminar for teaching, giving particular importance to shared university buildings such as library, central hall (with auditorium) and sports hall. As the colleges were also faculties, the need for separate teaching buildings was largely avoided. The rational order of the academic plan led naturally to the use of system construction. Without great variation in provision (except for the central shared buildings) the benefits of prefabrication could be exploited. CLASP provided visual consistency between the parts, speed of construction and a level of quality control. However, the lack of variation permitted in system building and the low budget level, prohibiting the use of marble chippings in the concrete aggregate which would have given greater whiteness and a sparkle in sunshine, led to a drab campus. Added to this the space between buildings consisted of long walkways because of the need to give each college an identity within the landscape. Unlike in Oxford or Cambridge where town streets provided attractive routes between colleges, at York there are open windy walkways. Admittedly a few old trees have been retained and many new ones planted, and the lake flows attractively against the sides of new buildings, but York shows the limits to rational, cost-cutting campus making.

Another British campus which gives priority to academic and architectural rationality is the University of Lancaster (1965). But here the rational and aesthetic have been combined. Major and minor dimensional grids unify all major planning decisions and relate academic and physical campus organisation. The centre of the Lancaster campus is a pedestrian spine only 5.5 metres wide which provides a dense linear focus for student interaction. The architect Gabriel Epstein argued that the spine should be fairly narrow to concentrate social life without congestion. All major buildings and activities (lecture theatres, faculties, library etc) are reached from the spine which runs at right angles to a subterranean system of service roads. From the spine, angled incidentally upon the axis of the historic town of Lancaster, spread a series of branches to faculty buildings which are themselves extendible laterally. These are not randomly arranged but subject to the discipline of a separate grid. All buildings are on a module of 10.6 metres wide (for natural light and ventilation) with alternative 30.5-metre wide college 'quads' and 30.5-metre wide spaces for access roads and parking areas[3]. As a consequence the nature and dimension of spines and spaces provides an indispensable link to the chain of knowledge at Lancaster. The arrangement is rational but hardly devoid of interest or character, with the routes and external quads reinforcing the curriculum not obstructing the flow of intellectual inquiry.

In many ways the rigour behind Shepheard Epstein's plan at Lancaster mirrors that of Jefferson's at the University of Virginia. Both place a pedestrian promenade at the centre and, by using a spine and lateral branches, allow for the exchange of ideas between students studying different disciplines. Rational planning at Lancaster has not produced a 'place-less' campus but one whose sense of place is related to the curriculum as against the wider landscape. Whereas Spence at Sussex and Lasdun at East Anglia forged a sense of place for learning out of the geography of location and monu-

mentality of forms, at Lancaster, and to some extent York, the character of the campus is driven by the internal logic of their respective universities.

A Case Study of Picturesque Grouping

Kobe Institute, Osaka, Japan

The Kobe Institute, designed in 1995 by Troughton McAslan (now John McAslan and Partners), is a distant residential annex of St Catherine's College, Oxford. Located overlooking Osaka Bay in Japan the Kobe Institute provides one-year postgraduate courses for Japanese graduates but taught in English by Oxford dons. The Institute follows the residential arrangement of Oxbridge: interlocking cloistered courts counterbalanced by larger teaching buildings – lecture hall, library, chapel. The design resolves well the demands of tradition and modernity.

The Kobe Institute uses an existing building (extensively refurbished) to form the backcloth to new residential wings. The older building, although undistinguished, gives scale to the whole and with conversion provides the main teaching accommodation. Parallel to this block Troughton McAslan placed an internal street flanked on the outer edge by four linked pavilions of student accommodation. In total there are forty-eight study bedrooms, each with *en suite* facilities, arranged on either side of an internal corridor which links the four blocks via staircases. On the lower floors are split-level lodgings for tutors; hence students and staff are housed collegiate fashion in the same building.

The wide internal street between the residential block and teaching accommodation provides a strict parallel geometry for the Institute. At right angles towards the west end a cross street leads to the main lecture theatre, its bulk being balanced to the east by a slender clocktower. The offset plan allows views outwards over the surrounding landscape, while providing a strong temple-like geometry for the whole.

Picturesque enclosure versus rational planning

3.8 Model, Kobe Institute, Japan, by Troughton McAslan. Notice the dialogue between rational building and informal landscape – the essence of the picturesque.

In detailed architectural treatment there is a large debt to Arne Jacobsen who designed the original St Catherine's College (1960) by successfully abstracting the traditions of the Oxford college. Troughton McAslan too have forged a hybrid of modernity and tradition, and East and West. The Kobe Institute is a multi-cultural education complex expressed in appropriate architectural language. It shows the benefit of upgrading an older building by careful grafting of new fabric, by mixing in dense format elements (teaching, residential, research) too often dispersed across the campus, and by combining the architectural languages of different cultures.

Building	Architect	Special Features	Cost
Kobe Institute, Japan	Troughton McAslan	• Skilful grafting of old and new • Exploits dramatic woodland site • Multi-cultural in style • Anchors design around clocktower	Total project cost £9 million in 1995

Notes

1. Tony Birks, *Building the New Universities,* David and Charles (1972), Newton Abbot, p 73.
2. Ibid, p 76.
3. Ibid, p 116. See also *Architectural Review,* April 1970.

Practical problems

Whatever type of masterplan is adopted, there remains the solving of fundamental practical problems. Of these the most pressing are circulation, creating room for external growth, defining the centre and campus edge, establishing the footprint of key buildings and environmental factors. Some have already been discussed but they require elaboration in order to set aesthetic criteria into the context of operational need.

Circulation

Three interacting systems of circulation exist on campus – service vehicles, car access and parking, and pedestrian movement. Many campuses suffer from the dominance attached to road vehicles, leaving pedestrians (and this usually means students) to struggle between parked cars and service yards. Well designed campuses give priority to pedestrian movement allowing wide and generous spaces for foot movement and relegating roads to minor areas to the rear of campus buildings. Unfortunately, many key policy makers at universities (deans, professors etc) demand car access almost to their office door and this forces roads to the centre of the campus. Rather like the opening up of rainforests by logging roads, once the road space is provided it is difficult to control use. Roads and their associated parking areas undermine the creation of the campus as a learning environment.

Pedestrian routes provide the necessary connection to lecture theatres, refectories and faculty buildings. The interconnections on the campus should be thought of as a web of foot-based circulation with nodes and sub-nodes at points of functional focus. The rhythm of movement on campus reflects both the layout of key buildings and the timing of lectures or tutorials. With modern modular programmes the time taken to walk from one lecture to another determines the configuration of the campus. With ten minutes between timed lectures (under slotted timetabling common in UK universities) the distance from one end of the campus to another cannot exceed about 500 metres. Pedestrian movement limits the size of the campus but helps establish the sense of grain and intensity of life.

4.1 Walking distance should limit the spread of the campus. Diagram from masterplan for the University of British Columbia, Vancouver, Canada.

4.2 Space standards for different types of pedestrian route from the University of British Columbia masterplan.

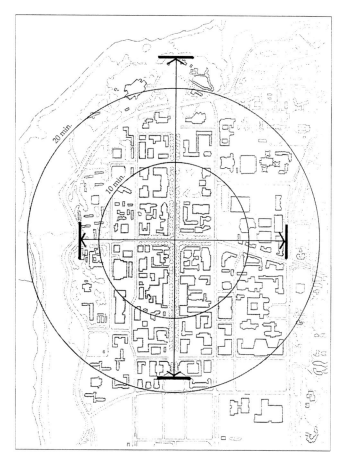

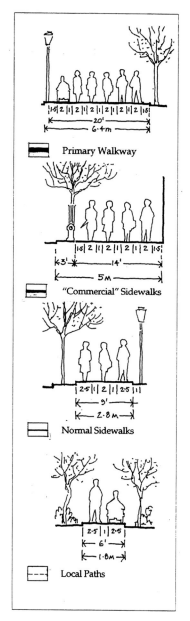

Walking on campus is the most efficient means of movement for students and academic staff. Routes should be direct, safe, clearly perceived, enjoyable to use, and reflective in spirit. Contact with nature is important, so too is the opportunity to engage in discussion away from the bustle of inter-lecture movement. Face-to-face contact, whether planned or accidental, is an important aspect of academic life. Routes need to help the flow of ideas by encouraging the interaction of students from different disciplines. Hence, key campus routes should not be internal to faculties or departments but shared external promenades edged by cafes, bookshops and student facilities. Roads where they exist should be external affairs, placed at the perimeter of the campus with their own connecting walkways from college car parks.

Service vehicles do necessarily need to reach the core of the campus. There needs to be provision for disabled access, for emergency vehicles, and for daily servicing of the estate. Generally, such provision is met by allowing some sharing of the road space with pedestrians. Strict controls are needed to avoid abuse by road vehicle users by installing barriers or speed humps and by allowing access only at certain times of the day. Since service vehicles have large turning circles their space needs can become out of proportion to the amount of land allocated to pedestrian (ie student) movement.

The design of circulation on the campus needs to provide permeability for students and access for vehicles. Students need to be able to filter through the gaps between the often large departmental buildings, and within the buildings themselves. They need variety of routes and a variety of types of space. Vehicles, on the other hand, need only one access point and little or no permeability across the campus. Large universities can accommodate different needs by employing a number of circulation levels (as in the design of the University of East Anglia by Denys Lasdun) and smaller universities can zone the land horizontally. Vertical segregation offers advantages but the environment can become alienating and sometimes dangerous. Dense interaction at ground level is the best strategy for foot movement.

If roads and circulation areas can be shared with pedestrians, the same is true of cyclists. Bicycle access is a common feature of modern campuses and helps to establish the identity of universities (eg Cambridge University in the UK, or Erasmus University in Holland). Encouraging cyclist movement helps reinforce the message of environmental stewardship which some universities are keen to promote (eg John Moore's University, Liverpool) but cycle access needs to be kept apart from pedestrian promenade areas. Cycles provide quick and efficient movement off campus but on campus controls are needed and good cycle storage is essential. Unlike cars which should not be allowed to penetrate to the campus centre, cyclists can be permitted to core areas as long as designated routes are provided.

The means of access whether on foot, cycle or car determines the size and density of the campus buildings. The decisions made with regard to types of masterplan (grid, linear, megastructure, collegiate etc) have direct consequences for circulation. However, it is better to decide

upon the grain and character of the university as an entity than to allow circulation to drive layout. Although the student is not often empowered to influence campus layout, it is student need which should determine the circulation system.

Inevitably, the means of circulation on the campus is influenced by the presence of transportation types off campus. Where public transport is well provided to the door of the

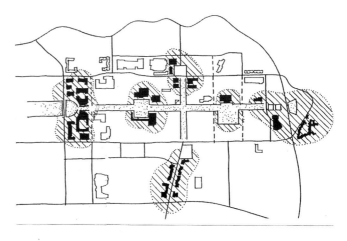

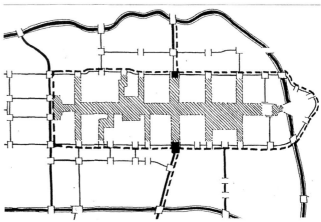

4.3 Space making should be related to pedestrian scale. Notice the way the formal composition (top) determines the road layout (bottom). Unversity of British Columbia, Vancouver, Canada.

4.5 Campus centre defined as social space and reinforced with tree-planting for shade (University of Newcastle, New South Wales, Australia).

university, there is less demand for car parking and road access. Many suburban universities have little alternative than to cater for high levels of car use by students and staff alike. Hence, conditions on campus can be most effectively improved by enhancing the quality of public transport in the vicinity of the university. Where tram or train services run nearby it makes sense to establish a university stop with its own footpath and lighting to the centre of the institution.

Many universities have between fifteen and twenty thousand students and staff, providing a level of demand which justifies the construction of a small station.

Universities have multiple entrances and multiform linkage. Facilities on campus are used by the town dwellers as well as the university community. Zoning movement and defining routes for different users is a key aspect of the campus plan. Rather than be isolated from the wider community there is the need for physical linkage to extend from the university centre to the campus edge and beyond to the town at large. Again the type and character of the plan influences the nature of these connections. An inward looking university with quiet tranquil spaces may promote high levels of intellectual inquiry but the isolation could damage the university in the long term.

4.4 'University' tram stop at California State University, Sacramento, USA.

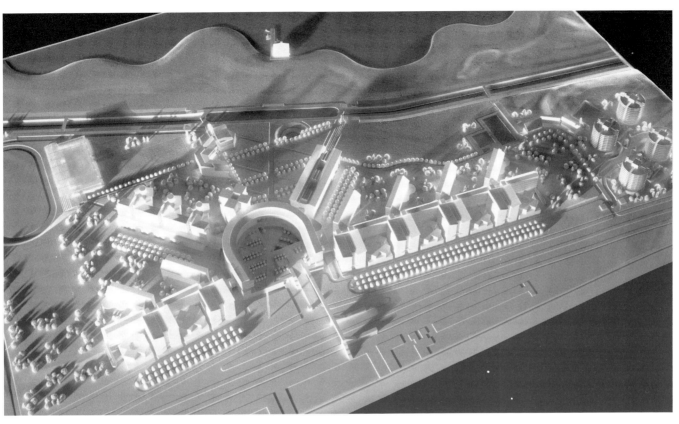

4.6 Campus planning as place making at Temasek Polytechnic, Singapore, by Michael Wilford and Partners.

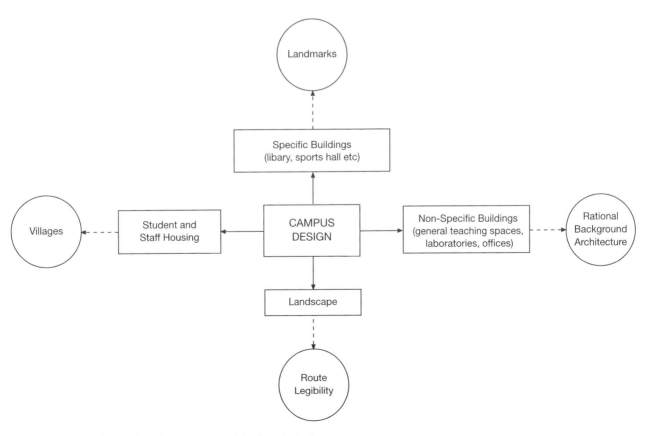

4.7 Main elements of the university campus and design strategies.

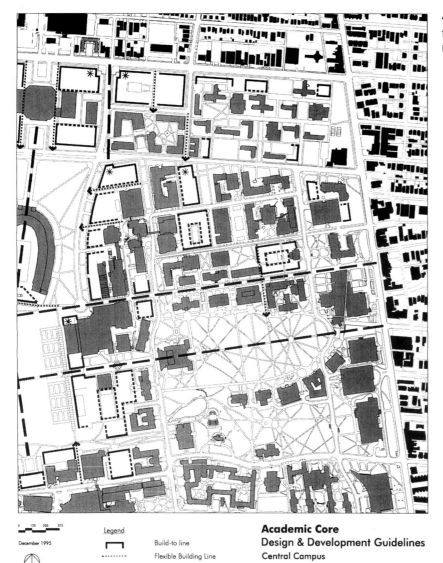

4.8 Defining the university centre through the fashioning of external space at Ohio State University, Columbus, USA.

0   125   250   375

December 1995

Legend

⌐¬ Build-to line

------ Flexible Building Line

* Landmark Feature

— — Visual Axis

·······➤ Pedestrian Route

Academic Core
Design & Development Guidelines
Central Campus

The Ohio State University
Campus Master Plan

Defining the centre

The role of the university masterplan is to promote communication between parts of the campus, to create adaptable yet coherent urban structures, and to provide the means of achieving a quality image for the university. The latter is largely fashioned by the nature of buildings and spaces which form the centre. Image is the result of memorable, vivid or coherent buildings grouped around lively, ordered or serene external spaces. Although architects tend to design buildings, it is the relationship between buildings and spaces which is the key to good campus design. This is particularly true of the university centre where setting, landscape and building design come together.

It is important that the university as a whole balances functional demands with aesthetic or sensual ones. Universities are places, small towns if you like, with their own identity. They are not placeless groups of anonymous buildings set within efficient gridded layouts, no matter how financially expedient such a solution can be. Creating a sense of place requires the forming of external space, its articulation through lively architecture and its animation by student life. It is 'place' which makes the university campus not 'building'. Unfortunately, the technical and functional demands of buildings tend to take priority over the creation and guardianship of the external or civic realm of the university.

The university centre is where the main buildings of the campus are grouped. Normally, the student union, library, vice-chancellor suite, refectory and graduation hall are located here. These activities should be allowed to enliven the edges of the space around which they are assembled, and to spill into it on certain occasions (graduation day, student rag week). University campuses bring into particular focus the difference between 'space' and 'place'. The latter requires people and

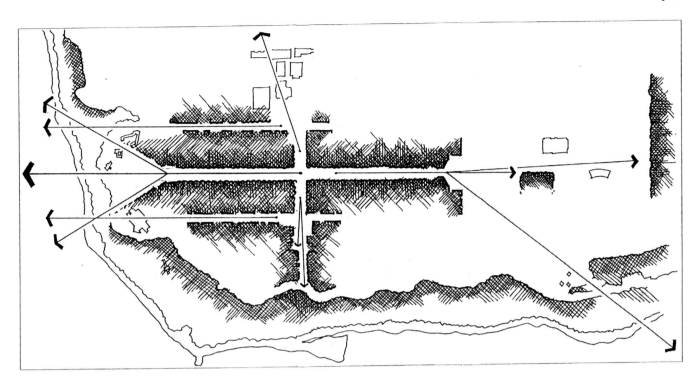

4.9   Views as a basis for campus planning. University of British Columbia, Vancouver, Canada.

memorable design, the former is abstract and lifeless. The university centre is a place in the full sense of the word, and the role of building and landscape design is to express its uniqueness and character.

Since the buildings which form the centre are large and distinctive, there is the tendency to elevate key buildings into campus landmarks. Defining the centre through place making and building punctuation are usually complementary activities. Skyline definition is often sought especially for the city-centre university where college buildings need to compete for attention in the urban scene. In 1925 C Z Klauder undertook a project for the new University of Pittsburgh proposing a sky-scraper called a 'Cathedral of Learning' inspired by the *Chicago Tribune* competition of three years earlier. Although Klauder's design was not built, it helped pave the way for high-rise campus buildings, especially in the United States.

There are many configurations for the formation of the university centre (linear, quadrangle, megastructure) but the deliberate fashioning of external space is essential. The key buildings which edge the space are each different in form and function, yet together they create the ensemble of volumes or activities which transform the space into a real place. The composition of the buildings as a group is important since visual identity remains the main element of perception. The centre needs to be defined by building volume, using profile, facade and set-back, to distinguish the academic centre from other parts of the campus.

The university centre is rarely formed by complete enclosure of external space, or regularity in the design of the individual buildings. More likely, there is a loose formation of individual structures, a slight irregularity of plan which adds subtlety to the composition. Within the group, dominance may be afforded to the library or learning resources centre, a prominent location given to the university bookshop, but generally it is the rhythm of human activity against the back-cloth of buildings which defines the centre. This activity should extend to an external processional space where graduates can be photographed in their gowns and where other cere-monial activities can be undertaken in dignified surround-ings. The linear nature of procession leads frequently to a longitudinal bias in the setting of the main campus buildings. The corridor of space created facilitates good communica-tion along its length, provides an avenue of debate for schol-ars walking to their next lecture, and, if free of cars and well planted, provides a memorable setting for the university.

A distinction is necessary between place making and establishing routes across the campus. A good masterplan sets down a sequence of external spaces which provide the development framework for individual buildings. The build-ings themselves define the spaces by giving physical enclo-sure, by establishing their social life, and by delineating secondary routes. The spaces are needed irrespective of roads and footpaths. It is better to establish a footprint of linked spaces on the campus and then to plumb the roads in later. This principle is particularly true of the campus centre.

Skyline

To many people the presence of the university is signalled by its distinctive skyline. Towers and spires have traditionally land-

4.10   Senate House (1932) by Charles Holden, University of London, UK.

4.11   Sather Tower by John Galen Howard, University of California, Berkeley, USA.

4.12   Burton Tower (1932) by Albert Khan, University of Michigan, Ann Arbor, USA.

4.13   Lurie Tower (1997) by Charles Moore, University of Michigan, Ann Arbor, USA.

48

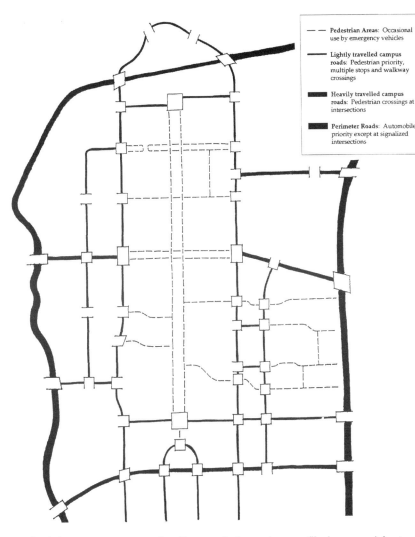

4.14 Campus edge defined by roads and gateways, University of British Columbia, Vancouver, Canada.

marked the campus, reserving the most shaped or profiled building to symbolise the centre. Many such towers litter the history of university architecture where their justification resides in the need for a conspicuous clock to ensure students attend lectures on time, a bell tower to signal prayer or meal times, or as a legacy of monastic origins. Today the tower is often more symbolic than functional (eg twenty-two storey Arts Tower at the University of Sheffield) though elevation is sometimes justified on the basis of privacy, the claimed intellectual benefits of fresh air and view, and the land costs in central areas.

High building is a feature of the twentieth-century campus. Height, however, is no guarantee of architectural distinction and a cursory glance at Cambridge or Harvard suggests that the most prominent university buildings are by no means the tallest. Skyline punctuation is a matter of profiling, of relationship between buildings and urban space, and of matching symbolic weight with functional hierarchy.

If a university campus needs an external point reference then some care needs to be devoted to high-building policy. Landmarking by tall buildings can be achieved by a single prominent tower, by a collection of towers or spires, and by using engineering or landscape elements as verti-

cal features. Too often, however, tall buildings are merely dominant structures without having the necessary distinction of form to ensure they achieve visual prominence. In the public mind it is shape and profile which leads to effective skyline punctuation, not bulk and size. Worse still, many cherished campus landmarks from the past have been bullied by new and poorly considered high buildings (eg Glasgow University where the impact of George Gilbert Scott's gothic skyline has been undermined by later buildings).

To be effective the landmark building requires a zone of unencumbered external space. Surrounding buildings should be kept fairly low so that the tower rises without visual competition. Ideally, the landmark should be seen in relationship to the ground, perhaps with a square at its base. The best campus landmarks enjoy singularity: there is no skyline competition and the tower itself, through its shape, colour, texture and proportion, is a worthy design. Certain landmarks work well with clarity of form, others benefit from complexity. The issue for the campus designer is whether the landmark is in the right place, has appropriate profile and contrast with its background, and is signalling an important element or place on the university estate.

4.15 Landscape design helps establish boundaries on campus. Ohio State University, Columbus, USA, sketch from masterplan by Sasaki Associates and Michael Dennis Associates.

Skyline punctuation helps locate the university in the urban scene and acts as a distance marker. As the campus is approached the landmark grows in size and often other structures come into view. Hence it is important that the vertical element can be seen on approach roads, sometimes as a terminating feature, or at other times as a fragment above tree or rooftops. The landmark needs to be designed to serve two distinct roles: that of university symbol on campus and as an external point reference in the cityscape.

Sometimes weak landmarks need the support of adjoining towers to perform their task. Single landmarks are not always distinctive enough, especially where their clarity of image has been compromised by poorly located new buildings. There are occasions when a group of towers can in an additive fashion add to the landmarking of the whole (eg MIT campus, Cambridge, Massachusetts, or North-western University, Chicago). The clustering of towers with a hint of competition has a pedigree at Oxford University, and is a useful strategy today for campuses where building height is inevitable. In such circumstances it is important that the whole takes on the characteristics of the single landmark building, and that in the ensemble of towers prominence of form reflects functional concentration.

Defining the edge

The campus is a distinct urban unit; a district devoted to higher education. As with all districts there needs to be a definition of centre, of edge, and an expression through buildings of functional uniqueness. The university district (or campus) requires its own landmarks, own spaces, and its own well-marked perimeter. The edge can be established in a variety of ways – through planting design, the physical marking of edge by buildings, the use of security gates onto the campus, or by the use of encircling roads. With rural or suburban universities the edge is usually defined by tree belts sometimes with secondary boundaries of hedges. The trees may blend into wooded copses or stitch the university into the external landscape of fields, woods and gardens.

With the urban university the problem of edge is more difficult to handle. Security and safety often require strong physical enclosure (with walls or buildings) and the use of security gates onto the campus. Such assertive physical separation may give those within the citadel of the university a feeling of security but the physical and psychological links to the town will be damaged. A balance has to be struck between defining the campus edge and linkage to the wider world. Edges are best delineated by perception barriers rather than physical ones, and where privacy is required, water or thorny planting are preferable to boundary walls.

Gates onto the campus may be marked by manned barriers or by softer means such as ramps, changes in paving material or doorless gates. As a district of the town the

Three Typologies	Examples
Big buildings/large spaces	Library
	Sports hall/stadium
	Congregation/senate hall
	Teaching hospital
Medium buildings/medium spaces	Faculty blocks
	Research laboratories
	Lecture theatres
	Refectory
Small buildings/small spaces	Halls of residence
	Gate lodges
	Bookshop/bank

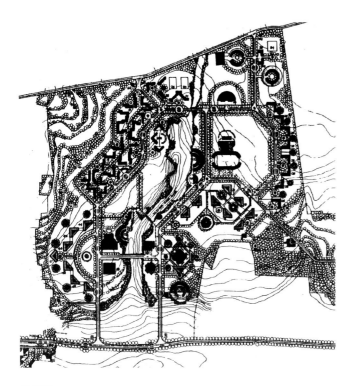

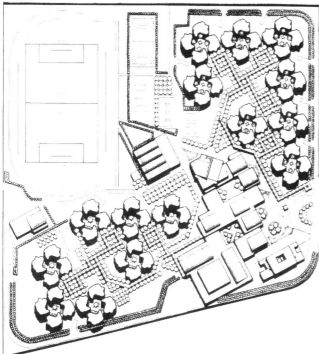

4.17   University of Blida, Algeria, masterplan by Skidmore, Owings and Merrill.

university requires the student or visitor to have a sense of the edge of the campus. It is rarely necessary to gate a university and arguably it is undesirable to do so in social or academic terms. Defining the edge is a question of establishing the boundary of where intellectual inquiry dominates all other pursuits.

Many universities define the campus boundary with a gateway building of some substance. Rather than construct a lodge, the large gateway building heralds the type of architecture and learning environment to be encountered in the centre of the university. Here the building signals to the centre and defines the edge. Its role is symbolic and through the approach to design should gesture towards the values of the university. A recent example is the Ruskin Library constructed in 1998 as a new gateway building to the University of Lancaster built initially in 1962.

Establishing the footprint of key buildings

Like many institutional estates the university campus consists of major and minor buildings. There are normally three distinctive typologies of buildings present and a corresponding taxonomy of exterior space.

The analysis of most campus plans confirms the presence of functional and spatial hierarchies. As the university grows the clarity of the three-stage order sometimes disintegrates.

Of the three main scales of building, growth is accommodated in quite different ways. Big buildings tend to grow by outward expansion, utilising external space set aside normally for other purposes like parking. Medium buildings grow by addition; a block of four lecture theatres may become six. Growth here is incremental and additive. With small buildings growth is usually by colonisation of undeveloped land – sometimes at the campus edge, sometimes at the centre. Another characteristic of growth is the way, with large buildings, expansion is normally accompanied by substantial internal modification, while with medium or smaller sized buildings growth is mainly by outward expansion.

The consequences for campus layout are threefold. First, big specialised buildings are best unencumbered by other structures, thereby providing the external space necessary for change. This was the pattern established at Berkeley in 1899 under the direction of Bernard Maybeck who advised on the campus competition plan. Second, where incremental growth is anticipated (as in research parks or student housing) there should be land available

Practical problems

4.18 Campus layout. University of California, Davis, USA, the Shields Library is right of centre.

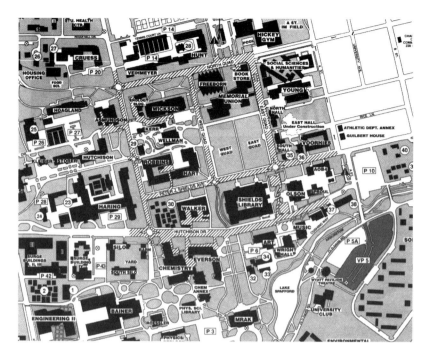

to form self-enclosing clusters with their own identity. Third, the expansion of medium sized faculty buildings provides the means of linking the scale of big buildings with the more informal groupings of the small ones. Their role may be to form physical connection or to support the perception of an organised whole.

The footprint of individual buildings is largely fashioned by the amount of accommodation needed. A library for six million volumes will clearly be a great deal bigger than one for half a million, but the principle of separation remains true. Even a small university library needs to grow, and growth is a factor of university life, especially in the areas which directly support teaching and learning.

Campus administrators often find themselves pressured to 'shoe-horn' unrelated minor buildings into the spaces left originally for the expansion of major ones. This happened with Maybeck's plan at Berkeley where growth of the Doe Library had to be achieved underground because of the presence nearby of later less significant campus buildings. Footprint is often larger than the actual buildings constructed in the early phases of an institution's life, yet footprint sacrifice is a common feature of university planning.

As a general rule the footprint on the ground for large and medium sized buildings should exceed initial expectations by 40 per cent. This allows growth to occur without disruption bearing in mind the longevity of typical university buildings (fifty to one hundred years). It is a feature of university life that change is rapid, unpredictable and resource demanding. Space on campus needs to reflect this.

Orderly growth is accommodated by establishing simple rectangular development parcels. These serviced by gridded or radial infrastructure networks (roads, service mains, fibre optics) and linked to strong pedestrian movement systems

provide the basis for much campus layout. Irregular pockets of land do not lend themselves to development for major buildings though they are well suited to more minor purposes such as student housing. Since the large buildings are normally at the campus centre, it is the smaller ones, such as research facilities, university farms or student villages which define the edge. At the University of California, Davis, the footprint of buildings (and their height) increases in size from the perimeter to the centre of the campus giving

4.19 Campuses are computing environments, high-tech gateways for local communities. California State University, Chico, USA.

4.20 Place making using lawns and trees at the Stephen Hawking Institute, University of Cambridge, UK, by Edward Cullinan and Associates.

clarity to the conception. Here the Shields Library, occupying nearly a whole block on the gridded layout, anchors the whole composition physically and academically.

Computing on campus

Most universities are computing environments. The range, use and variety of computers on campus is a useful measure of a university's vitality. Over the past two decades, universities have helped lead the change to a digital society working often with research institutions to develop new forms of computing hardware and software. Many universities have their own high speed computer networks linking workstations on and off campus. At Stanford University, for instance, SUNet connects 25,000 host computers, microcomputers and workstations on campus to national super-computer centres, the Internet and World Wide Web. All students and staff have immediate access to electronic mail, department information, course web pages and personal filing systems. In fact,

4.21 Strong landscape framework enhances the setting for academic life (University of Newcastle, New South Wales, Australia).

4.22 The landscape of education at Unversity of California, Berkeley, USA.

at Stanford and other universities in the USA such as MIT, students are not required to own their computers. They have computer clusters in halls of residence (both undergraduate and postgraduate) and research registered students automatically receive their own computer at their study centre.

The cabling needs of such provision presents a problem on existing campuses although they can be readily met in new buildings. Taking fibre-optic cabling through the fabric of older buildings is necessarily disruptive and expensive. Once achieved stability does not long remain for the speed of change in computing is rapid. Accessibility to cabling and network points is essential, leading often to raised floors in science laboratories and exposed perimeter trunking elsewhere.

Landscape design

If campus design is largely an exercise in place making then campus landscape has a significance at least as great as architectural design. The planted framework of many universities and the design of the intimate spaces between buildings is the means by which the disparate buildings of the typical university are united. The design of the external landscape involves establishing at the macroscale a coherent framework of tree belts, hedges, gardens, greens, playing fields, roads and parking areas which integrate the buildings and their external spaces into an imageable whole. The objective is to use landscape design to reinforce the sense of an academic district complete with vistas, containment, edges, gateways and spatial hierarchies. Planting of different types, using many species for their seasonal colour or texture, can complement the orchestration of built forms.

Many campuses are conceived along the lines of 'place making' by landscape design and 'place marking' by building design. This was the approach of Jefferson and Olmsted in America which Frank Lloyd Wright revived in his Florida Southern College designs of 1946. It remains a useful strategy since without a strong initial landscape framework the campus can degenerate into nothing but landmark buildings. Often the bones of landscape design already exist when a university acquires land for development. The inherited trees and woodland can then form part of the structure of landscape design (eg University of Exeter). Fresh planting is always needed, however, to establish the development parcels, vistas and campus edges for the new university. Since trees take time to mature, the full integration of building and landscape design is not usually achieved in the first generation of university development. During this

4.23 Trinity College, Oxford, from Loggan's view of 1675. Trees, gardens and courtyards are part of the tradition of campus design. Landscape should never be neglected at universities.

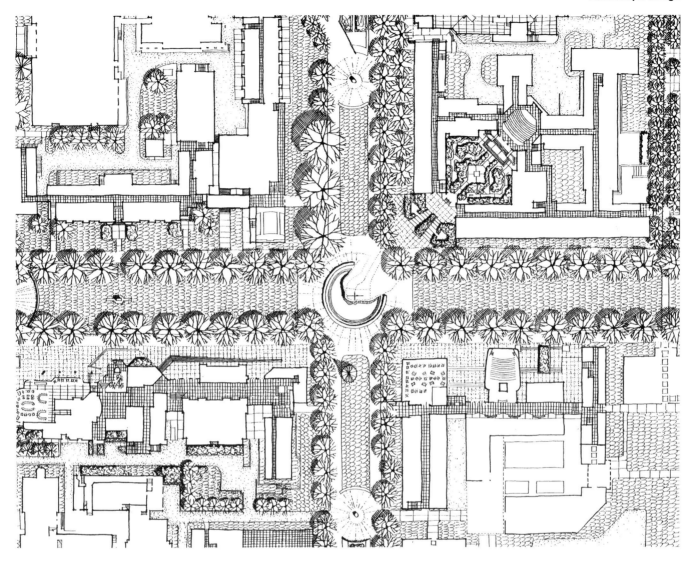

4.24 Design of space between buildings at the University of British Columbia, Vancouver, Canada.

period there is sometimes the tendency to sacrifice planted areas for new development, or to neglect the maintenance of the emerging and sometimes struggling vegetation.

Successful universities from the past have generally a fine inheritance of trees, gardens and paved quads. Here expert care is needed to protect and maintain these features since many are of historic as well as aesthetic value. The mature campus has a balance in scale and visual impact between planted areas and built ones (eg Trinity College, Dublin). Sometimes the gardens were created for medicinal purposes, and at other times for contemplation. These roles tend to be replaced today by the planting of arboreta which can be used for educational and social purposes.

Modern planting design is an exercise in creating large external rooms into which different types of development can take place. The rooms are joined together to form a sequence of big outdoor spaces, each with their own species of planting, modelling of contours and connecting vistas. The

4.25 Campus life, Student Union Square, University of Newcastle, New South Wales, Australia.

Practical problems

Hard, as against soft, landscape helps establish a sense of place around buildings allowing them to connect with each other effectively. The articulation of the spaces between buildings mediates between architectural and landscape design, providing the means of sequencing and signalling movement across the campus. Since most movement at a university is on foot, sometimes in great floods as between lectures, the spaces at the perimeter of buildings are corridors of movement.

The design and fashioning of external space needs to distinguish between routes used for movement and other areas such as paved courts used for student gossip. The internal functional spaces of buildings and the closely related external courts need to be designed in a unified fashion if students and staff are to be encouraged to engage in discussion between seminars. Here, besides paths, steps and ramps, there will be terraces, pools, seats and fountains, perhaps with pleated limes or beech trees for shelter or shade.

The textures and colours introduced to the campus through landscape design can contrast, complement or unify those employed in the buildings. Two approaches are common: either to restrict the palette of landscape design allowing a variety of colours and textures of buildings to add distinctiveness (Cambridge University) or to unify the buildings allowing the landscape elements to provide sparkle (Princeton University). Time obscures the differences and adds a healthy complexity but landscape design and building design cannot be seen as unrelated activities.

whole composition is given a strong edge which may be marked by a particular type or scale of tree at entry points, with the overall design merging into the wider landscape in a natural fashion. Even when there is no great natural context as in the inner-city campus, landscape design should form a major element of the campus masterplan. Here planting could establish an island of greenery which will help identify the university and give it a distinctive image in what is maybe a broader landscape of dereliction.

At the finer level, the design of paths, roads, courtyards and terraces plays an important part in defining functional zones or key routes, and gives clues to campus territory.

It is true to say that the university campus is both landscape and landmark. Landscape alone does not make a place of higher learning although it effectively creates an ambience of learning. Building design too fails to create on its own a campus in the widest sense. Landscape and landmark are related – two poles engaged in the forging of identity and image. At one level they signal to outsiders the presence of the university, at another in a semiotic sense they give students a symbol of learning, and in an educational way the buildings and landscapes are part of the learning experience.

Landscape in particular has a role to play in bringing nature into students' lives. As society faces ever greater environmental stress, the stewardship of the land and the

4.27 Landscape and landmark through public art at University of California, Davis, USA.

4.28   Constable Terrace, University of East Anglia, Norwich, UK. Low-energy student housing by Rick Mather.

resources of nature can be brought effectively to student attention through the design of the campus landscape. Nature has the potential to be both an inspiration to thought and to provide paradigms of sustainability. To confront students with these issues in their university days prepares them for the ecological challenges of life.

Environmentalism on the campus

In 1992 the UK government published a report chaired by Professor Peter Toyne, Vice-Chancellor of Liverpool John Moore's University, entitled *'Environmental Responsibility: an Agenda for Further and Higher Education'*.[1] Responding to the Rio Summit of the same year, the report argued that the university campus should present an example to students and the wider community on how the problems of global warming, ozone depletion and the maintenance of biodiversity could be addressed. The university was seen as providing a unique opportunity to demonstrate the benefits of environmental design while also engendering in the students' mind the importance of ecological choices through different educational programmes.

The Toyne Report promulgated the view that everybody from vice-chancellor to student should have some scope on campus for developing a more ecologically sound approach to living. The campus was seen as a testbed for new environmental technologies, new styles of living,

working and studying, and for new approaches to transportation. The benefit of the report was its all embracing nature: it addressed campus layout, building design, the means of moving about campus, waste management, paper procurement, energy systems and extended into the importance of giving all students a grasp of green issues through degree programmes even in non-environmental subjects. For instance, Toyne argued that the teaching of English or History could be couched at least in part in ecological terms in order to achieve 'cross-curriculum greening'.

While the Toyne Report gives weight to the need for an environmentally knowledgeable and skilful workforce through different kinds of educational programme, its significance to campus architects was the expectation that green ideas should be tested or demonstrated in the new buildings constructed or in the way existing buildings were managed. Design had a central role to play in reinforcing the green message. Universities were encouraged to adopt 'comprehensive environmental policy statements' linked to action plans involving the whole campus estate. Sound environmental practice was seen as essential to future needs and held the benefit of allowing universities to become less expensive to run especially in terms of energy and other utility bills. Environmentalism was also advocated as enhancing a university's reputation with its region, thereby improving recruitment and public image.

The Toyne Report spawned no new campuses but did lead to a number of innovative green building projects at UK universities. Typical among them is the Queens Building at De Montfort University in Leicester which not only explores but demonstrates to engineering students the benefits of natural solar-assisted ventilation in a science building. Another project at the University of Northumbria utilises photovoltaic panels as an overcladding system for an earlier computer building. At the University of East Anglia, the Elizabeth Fry Building (for a Social Science Department) applies a system of low-energy design based upon groundwater cooling while nearby Constable Terrace, a block of student housing, tests another approach to ecological design. These projects flowed from the Toyne

4.29 South Bank University, new campus at Elephant and Castle, London, UK, by Building Design Partnership. The design seeks to revive an inner-city area.

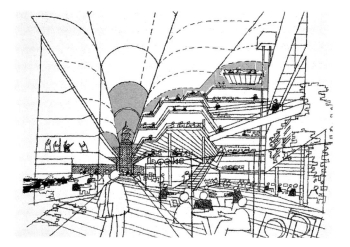

Report's recommendations with the result that more green buildings are located on university campuses than elsewhere in the UK.

The problem of the inner-city campus

Universities in inner cities face particular difficulties. The sense of decline as old industries collapse or housing areas deteriorate, the rise in crime and vandalism, the under-achievement in feeder schools or colleges, all add to the university's problems. The university is, however, often the major employer and investor in new buildings in such areas. Furthermore, its academics and students hold the key to the regeneration of the inner city by the skills taught and new knowledge imparted. This sense of renewal through the vehicle of the university needs to find expression in the design of buildings and spaces.

Often as inner cities decline extra government grants are directed to those universities affected. This provides the money to regenerate older, sometimes historic buildings, to create new landmarks to signal regeneration, and to establish training programmes to re-skill the workforce. The systematic rebuilding of the worn-out industrial city can begin with the university taking a role in both physical and intellectual renewal. Since universities are able to attract public and private funds they can be effective catalysts of change.

Site planning and building design are key elements in the process. The university masterplan may need to adjust to external circumstances beyond the campus edge, to exploit for instance land and buildings which have become vacant in the neighbourhood. New sites create the opportunity to forge fresh linkages with the external web of urban activity. The chance may occur to create a direct route to public transport provision, to open up views of a riverside or to create a fresh urban park around which new academic buildings can be located. The physical and human assets of the inner city may be revived by the university using funds directed at the region for urban renewal.

Frequently, the pattern of industrial change in the inner city is to move from heavy engineering to a service

4.30 Car park as campus monument at Stanford University, Palo Alto, USA.

4.31 Successful definition of edge and entry. Kochi University of Technology, Japan.

4.32 Masterplan for Harrow campus, University of Westminster, UK, by RMJM. Notice how the buildings are separated in order to facilitate phased development.

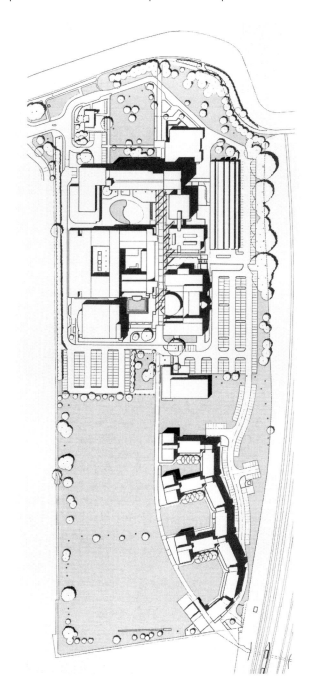

industry economy. The new jobs and business units tend to be in the high-tech field, and this pattern of change is often echoed in the university where, for instance, a textiles engineering department will be replaced by a fashion design department. The estate of the university will not only reflect these changes, but in a sense lead them. Where this happens the new buildings for computer or media studies will act as beacons of regeneration.

One of the problems of the inner city is that fully cleared sites are rarely available. The campus and its hinterland will consist of pockets of development, quite well formed urban groupings surrounded by land perhaps contaminated by earlier industrial uses. Isolated parcels of existing development may exist compromising the clean sweep of urban reform. This makes forward planning difficult, yet the remaining structures often have value economically or aesthetically. The challenge for the designer is to work with these structures creating in the process greater continuity and pleasant contrast between old and new buildings. The existence of buildings, streets and industrial structures needs to inform design on the campus either by clever association or by marking a sharp change in outlook.

With piecemeal change on and off the campus, it is difficult to achieve an all-embracing order. Opportunity needs to be grasped but the consequences on the whole ought not to be ignored. New buildings may enhance the image of the university and provide valuable space for teaching fresh skills, but the sense of order in the masterplan should not be compromised for short-term economic advantage. It is the external space pattern of the campus which tends to be the main giver of character and which endures the longest. The courtyards, processional routes and landscaped grounds need to be preserved and added to via the process of urban regeneration. Opportunities should be taken when constructing new buildings to form fresh linkages campus spaces.

Car parking is a major environmental problem on many inner-city campuses. A university of fourteen thousand students has typically a thousand staff. Assuming that half of these and about 5 per cent of students use cars

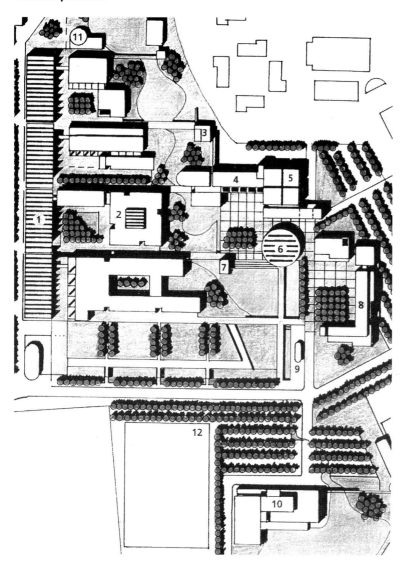

4.33 Central area, University of Phuket, Thailand, by RMJM. Key: 1 General Teaching, 2 Faculty Space, 3 Medical Centre, 4 Student Centre, 5 Multi-purpose Hall, 6 Library, 7 Spirit House, 8 Administration Building, 9 Security, 10 Sports Centre, 11 Crèche, 12 Sports Pitches.

to reach the university, then a thousand parking spaces are required. This would consume about 3 hectares of land – an area sufficient to house about a thousand students in halls of residence. So for every parking space there is the loss of approximately one student residence on campus. Surface car parking is an environmental eyesore, takes land better used for other purposes and is the single most important factor in the destruction of collegiate character.

The university campus is often an island of order in a sea of disorder. It is common for the campus island to be reinforced by new perimeter development with gateways and control points. These are often justified by the presence of crime and vandalism off campus. Students have a right to a safe and secure environment but the fortified campus mitigates against social or community interaction. Town and gown share more common objectives than the form of some inner-city campuses would suggest. External linkage with the definition of edge achieved by perceptual means is preferable to physically closed perimeters.

Funding and implementation

Generally speaking university projects consist of:

(a)   New campus masterplans and related buildings.
(b)   The refurbishment and enlargement of existing university campuses.
(c)   The provision of new buildings in existing universities, many of which are of historic interest.

In order to implement university expansion in developed and third world locations it is important that architects are familiar with the grants available from agencies such as the World Bank, United Nations and charities. In the UK and Europe acquaintance with the financial regimes of the EU, Lottery and HEFCE (Higher Education Funding Council for England) is important, in the USA similar aid is provided via federal and state higher education agencies. Increasingly, in both the developed and third world, the ability to attract private sector funding is crucial. Architects have, therefore, to be able to advise on funding issues when projects are under consideration.

Implementation of projects in terms of the method of procurement has become increasingly complex as contractors have become progressively the lead representative of the client. Architects may be involved in fresh ways, acting perhaps as the client's representative in monitoring contractor performance, or by becoming part of the contractor's team subsequent to developing outline design proposals. Often too architects are part of multi-disciplinary practices, offering to university clients a consortium of expertise from engineering to landscape and contracting services. Some international practices such as Ove Arup and Partners and RMJM in the UK, HOK and SOM in the USA, team up readily with local contractors or have good working relationships with global contracting companies such as Kvaerner. For the client the main concerns are cost, time and quality – architects have necessarily to address all three in the demanding environment of building procurement for the higher education sector.

Two Case Studies of New Universities on the Pacific Rim

(a) *University of Phuket, Thailand: a case study of
     landscape and growth*

In 1996 RMJM was appointed to prepare a master-plan for Rangsit International University on a 50-hectare site, with views to the Indian Ocean, at Phuket in Thailand. The plan is essentially a spatial, land-use and circulation concept to allow a new university of ten thousand students to grow in self-contained phases while producing a coherent whole on completion. The objective is to produce a stimulating environment for teaching, learning and research using densely built forms and a rich pattern of open space in order to create a sense of an academic community.

Five possible configurations were considered – urban collegiate, campus collegiate, radial, linear and dispersed – and tested against the demands of climate, qualities of site, programme and cultural traditions of this part of South-East Asia. The final form owes much to a blending of the advantages of urban collegiate and linear. Landscape design plays an important role in

moderating the effects of a hot climate and in giving character to the external realm.

The masterplan objectives of phased growth, order and clarity of route have been met by giving priority to pedestrian movement, by employing a close grain of buildings, by establishing a landscaped spine through the campus, and by establishing a clear identity for the centre. In the latter the main university buildings are located: library, sports hall, faculty lecture theatres, student and medical centre, congregation hall and administration. The centre is dense with closely set rectangular buildings arranged around planted courtyards and canals. Space for growth exists at the perimeter of each building, but the need for future expansion does not jeopardise the essential collegiate character of the whole. General teaching space and halls of residence occur as a ring around the centre, allowing the development to grade evenly into the wider landscape.

Whereas the framework establishes a centre of interlocking courtyards, the organisational geometry is mainly linear. Running through each court is a street which acts as a planning grid for services and main-

4.34 Kochi Technical University, Japan, designed by Nikken Sekki Architects.

tains a spatial discipline across the whole. Being essentially linear, the development can expand laterally allowing phasing to take place in an orderly fashion.

Like many new campuses, vehicles have a secondary role. The centre is for students not cars, and trees not parking spaces. Formal planting and lawns give a traditional academic character to the centre and help reinforce the relationship, so typical of good university environments, between internal and external space and between collective order and personal space. Planting is designed to delineate key routes across the campus and to provide shade for pedestrians.

Circulation routes for vehicles are not allowed to penetrate to the campus 'core' and where roads exist there is extensive traffic calming. The slope across the site has been exploited to place parked cars beneath decks, utilising the roofs in part as sports pitches. Electric vehicle servicing exists in the centre (as it does at UC Davis) with space shared with pedestrians without separate zoning. Pedestrian routes across the campus are designed to establish academic nodes at about five minutes walking distance, with rest and meet points every minute or so along key routes.

(b) *Kochi Technical University, Kochi, Japan: reviving the clocktower as academic emblem*

The new 50,000 square metre campus at Kochi in Japan, designed by Nikken Sekkei Architects (1997), consists of seven faculty buildings placed in a loose classical grouping around a clocktower and observation point. The layout is based around interlinked courtyards served by colonnaded walkways which focus upon the clocktower as an orientating feature. The architectural language blends East with West; there is a three-storey, brick-clad, basecourse above which rises a variable deck of green sheathed pavilions of oriental flavour.

The eleven-storey clocktower helps locate the new university in the wider Japanese landscape. It is slen-

Building	Architect	Special Features	Cost
Kochi Technical University, Japan	Nikken Sekkei	• Clocktower as central feature • Interlocking courtyards • Separate faculty buildings united by consistent language	Not available

der and topped by a glazed lantern which provides views outwards over the immediate campus. The tower helps mark the centre of the new campus and acts as a gateway to the administrative block. Nearby there are lecture theatres, classrooms, research facilities, laboratories, sports halls and student residences. Each block is a self-contained building whose form reflects the different functional requirements of higher education, yet each is united by a consistent architectural style and use of materials. There are three types of facing brick employed in conjunction with fair faced concrete or stone, with trim in anodised aluminium. The language, although subtlely different, gives each block a separate identity while unifying the whole.

The clocktower not only punctuates the composition, it gives a focus to the different buildings that rise from three-storeys high (halls of residence) to seven storeys (main teaching block). The horizontal spread of the main faculty buildings with their sweeping lawns is attractively counter-balanced by the elegant verticality of the clocktower. The precedents for this approach are the campuses of the USA, notably Berkeley and Stanford which also exploit skyline to signal the presence of an academic community.

Note

1. *Environmental Responsibility: an Agenda for Further and Higher Education,* Department for Education (1992), London.

Sustainable development and the campus

CHAPTER

5

Universities are well placed to develop new approaches to environmental design. Their mission of teaching excellence, open mindedness and research development coincides with both the development of the science base of sustainability and the pedagogic opportunities afforded by low-energy demonstration projects. The campus is a good place to start to instil in young people sound environmental practices. The procurement of services from paper to buildings provides the opportunity to explore recycling, to apply new energy technologies, and to test ecological approaches to estate management. The problems of global warming, ozone depletion and loss of biodiversity are all city related, and as such the university campus provides a neat microcosm in which better practices can be explored.

Many universities make reference to 'environmental responsibility' in their charters or mission statements. Since they are under less pressure to achieve profits than private companies, they are well placed to show that sustainable development is realisable within the cost limits of most forms of building procurement. Also as students are likely to be future clients, their education in the area of sustainability is crucial to the culture change facing society as a whole.

The delicate balance between nature and man is acted out on every university campus. How resources such as land, water, and fossil fuels are used; the extent of recycling or energy recovery; and the respect for ecology, are all indicators of a commitment to sustainability. The university can influence the environmental agenda in three ways:

(a) By putting environmental understanding into every course or programme at undergraduate level.
(b) By introducing specialist environmental qualifications at post-graduate level.
(c) By placing sustainability into the agenda of all aspects of the institution's life – from buildings to transport, landscape design to consumables.

This largely is the advice of the UK government report of 1992 *Environmental Responsibility: an Agenda for Further*

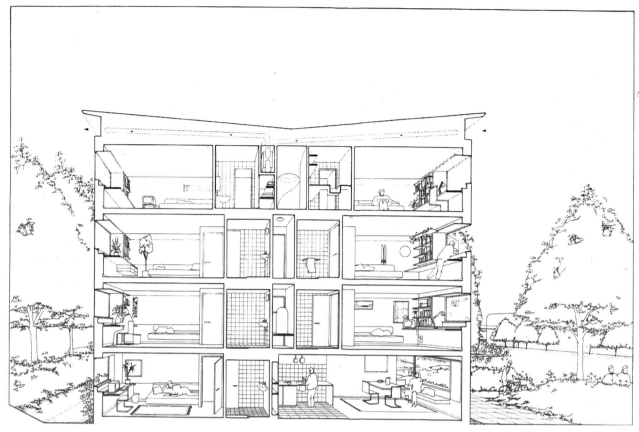

5.1 Section through low-energy student housing at Constable Terrace, University of East Anglia, Norwich, UK, by Rick Mather.

and *Higher Education* which led to further advice such as *Educated Energy: Good Housekeeping in Further and Higher Education Buildings* (DETR, 1998) and *Student Energy Awareness Scheme – University of East Anglia* (DETR, 1998). These different reports highlight the key role of senior management in taking advantage of special funding schemes for projects on campus which test and support the principles of sustainable development. In the case of the University of East Anglia the main players in an ambitious programme of low-energy projects were the estates officer, the head of finance and the student union representative. The financial savings achieved flowed to both the university and the students. The initiative focused upon halls of residence which, being built between 1962 and 1998, had varying degrees of energy efficiency. About a quarter of the university's annual energy bill was spent heating, lighting and ventilating student residences, amounting to about £500,000 per year. Due to a mixture of design and management changes, many involving the students themselves who for instance controlled heating controls and lights in their rooms, the university was able to make a saving of 8 per cent. As the savings were achieved mainly in the halls of residence, it was agreed that the benefits would flow to the students with the money being distributed via the student union.

Halls of residence are an obvious place to start in energy efficiency measures on campus. The national

energy bill in the UK for the 212,000 student residences is £35 million, representing about 25 per cent of the overall energy use in the higher education sector.[1] As heating student residences produces the equivalent of 135,000 tonnes of carbon per year, it is important to involve students themselves in the energy efficiency measures by appealing to their general environmental concerns. With education (preferably via the student union) students readily adopt better practices – such as turning off lights when the room is unoccupied and turning heating controls down rather than opening windows when the room becomes too hot – which can usefully compliment fabric or heating system improvements. The lessons of energy efficiency measures at the University of East Anglia are:

- the importance of targeting halls of residence
- the need to involve the student union
- the benefit of returning energy-efficiency profits to the students themselves
- the importance of combining energy upgrading with a parallel education programme.

Other universities have explored different routes to sustainability. Universities are complex organisations with a typical campus containing a variety of different types of building each with their own energy characteristics – laboratories, teaching space, offices, kitchens, sports halls, residences.

5.2   Solar panels on Tercero Building, University of California, Davis, USA.

Their scale means it is easy to assume that somebody else will take care of the sustainability costs in the area of enegy, water and other resources. Two practices are useful: the first, as has just been mentioned, is to involve students via the student union in conservation initiatives and to return some or all of the savings to them. The second is to devolve budgets so that faculties and departments pay their own energy and water bills. This helps motivate faculty staff and students in the financial benefits of good practice. The latter requires metering and monitoring at the finest practical level within the institution. Knowledge and motivation are the keys to good practice.

An example of the benefit of devolution of energy bills is with regard to sports halls. A typical university sports centre uses as much energy as fifty houses, mostly in lighting and heating. An optimum temperature is 15 °C but often sports halls are kept a degree or two warmer (for staff comfort) adding 6-10 per cent to the heating bill. Frequently too the lights are left on when the hall or courts are not in use adding further to energy wastage. Too rarely do showers or taps have regulators or timing controls, adding further to energy and water costs. A dripping tap can waste 10,000 litres of water per year and a hot dripping tap can cost nearly £2 per day in electricity. So by devolving budgets and monitoring performance, in giving staff knowledge of energy and water usage by metering at the point of use, efficiency can be enhanced by an estimated 10-20 per cent by good housekeeping alone.[2]

In energy efficiency matters the benefits are both real and can lead to an enhanced image. A university which presents the appearance of being environmentally concerned via the construction, for example, of low-energy student residences is likely to attract better staff and students, and to enjoy an enhanced reputation with the local community. Although difficult to quantify, there are long-term financial benefits of a good environmental image.

A typical large university uses enough electricity each year to drive an electric train for 2,735,300 kilometres, requiring over five million trees to convert the CO_2 produced back to oxygen.[3] Senior staff have a role to play in motivating support staff. They can appoint an energy manager, spread the ownership of energy matters through devolved budgets,

and by working with student representatives create a culture of environmental responsibility. A concern for sustainability – whether in the means of getting to or about campus, in the design of buildings or the maintenance and upgrading of the existing building stock – points to a university with a forward-looking agenda. Such universities are likely to be key players – not just in the higher education sector – but in re-fashioning lifestyles for the larger community.

The economic impact of universities: a chance to develop models of sustainability

Universities can have considerable economic impact on their town and the wider region. When visiting a university town (Cambridge in the UK, Aachen in Germany, UC Davis in California) the extent of economic and cultural vitality which the university brings is obvious. In fact, the smaller the town, the larger the university, the greater the impact. The growth in student numbers over the past decade means that in some towns the university is now the largest single employer, or it makes the greatest contribution to the region's economy. There exists the potential, therefore, to forge an alliance of sustainable development between city and university.

A recent case study of the town of Chico in Northern California highlights the impact. California State University,

5.3 Environmental design strategy at the Computer Centre, University of Sunderland, UK (top winter, below summer). Building Design Partnership.

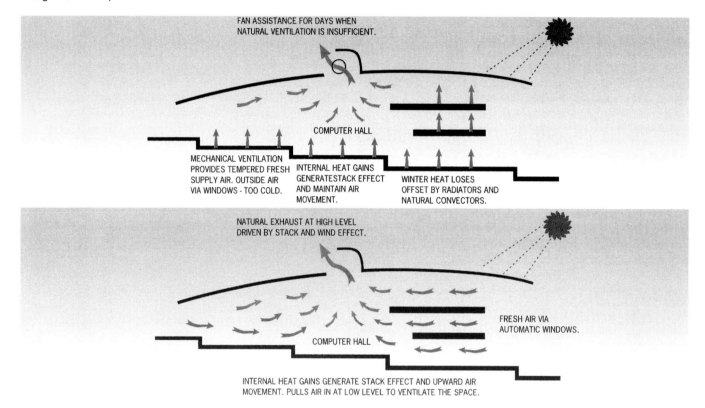

Chico (CSU,C) has about fourteen thousand students and nearly nine hundred faculty and other staff in a town of barely a hundred thousand. In 1995–96 employees and students spent $205 million in the region, broken down into:

- employee spending $60 million
- materials, construction, operating expenses $46 million
- student spending $99 million.

Although most of the money spent is the result of student fees or parental maintenance contributions, CSU,C receives also about $20 million each year in external grants of various kinds. Economists at the university estimate that every dollar spent in the community generates 2.2 times its amount in 'trickle down' before leaving the local area.[4] As a consequence the total annual economic impact is over $450 million. So for every resident in Chico the university generates an annual income of over $4,000, enough to develop new initiatives in the area of sustainability.

With such direct economic impact, universities can play a significant role in improving the quality of life and providing green services for the wider community. These create jobs directly, and, by the skills or enterprise generated, lead to further jobs outside the higher education sector. This is why universities located in city areas need particularly to address the community and sustainability interface, and why the town should create facilities such as business parks in order to maximise the potential economic regenerative effect of environmental expertise.

It is evident from Chico's experience that in relatively small towns, the economic impact of higher education is considerable. Putting aside the cultural, social and sustainability benefits, the financial rewards for a region far outweigh the disadvantages in terms of stress upon rented accommodation or traffic congestion. At Aachen, in Germany, there are over fourty thousand students in a town of only about 150,000 people. Here education is the prime source of employment and the major player in introducing green initiatives in areas such as transport to the region. In Huddersfield, in Northern England, a university of fifteen thousand students exists in a town of about a hundred thousand creating considerable economic benefits for a

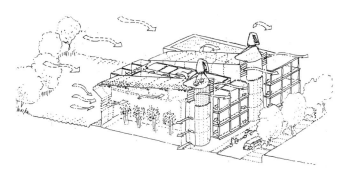

5.4   Electric campus vehicle at University of California, Davis, USA.

5.5   Diagram showing environment strategy at new campus, University of Nottingham, UK, by Michael Hopkins and Partners.

region once dominated by the textile industry. How it remodels itself around social and environmental sustainability will be a useful measure of its success as an academic institution.

Two Sustainability Case Studies:

(a)   New Campus, University of Nottingham, UK

In 1998 Michael Hopkins and Partners prepared a masterplan for a 6-hectare expansion of the University of Nottingham, using a redundant Raleigh bicycle factory site almost 2 kilometres from the main campus. The prominence given to green principles makes this project of particular importance. The approach has been described by the architect as 'eco-functionalism': a blending of ecological principles and those of space flexibility.[5]

The layout consists of parallel fingers of accommodation overlooking a lake which stores re-cycled grey water and provides chilled air for summer-time cooling. The lake is also a wildlife refuge and being on the south side of the development provides a sunny pedestrian promenade away from cars. The buildings, mainly flexible teaching accommodation, are placed at right angles to the lake with a combination of glazed atria and open courtyards between each block. The atria are an important aspect of the development. Besides providing heating through passive solar gain, the glazed malls naturally ventilate the buildings by exploiting the stack effect. At the top of each atrium is a wind tower which aids air movement and draws the stale air out of adjacent lecture theatres and staff rooms. The atria are also social spaces: places where students and staff can meet informally within a sheltered semi-external environment.

The lake, angled atria, shallow plan depth teaching space and toast rack layout are all the result of

5.6   Model, new campus, University of Nottingham, UK, by Michael Hopkins and Partners.

5.7 Section, Science Faculty, University of Cyprus, by Mario Cucinella with Andreas Kyprianou.

environmentaly conscious design. At a detailed level the project tests new forms of construction such as a low pressure drop ventilation system (for which an EU demonstration grant of £740,000 was obtained), heat recovery technology, and photovoltaic driven air-handling units. Built at a cost of £845 per square metre, the project is not expensive by higher education standards. Sustainability here produces a distinctive development which helps establish the agenda for the next century in the minds of students.

(b)   Science Faculty, University of Cyprus, Nicosia

Occupying an area of 14,500 square metres, the new £6.5 million science building at the University of Cyprus (1998) exploits innovative environmental design as a demonstration to students of using science to reduce dependence upon air-conditioning in hot climates. Designed by Mario Cucinella Architects with Andreas Kyprianou Associates, the approach is one of courtyards and shallow depth building. The new faculty is designed as a series of parallel buildings on either side of an open shaded spine of palm trees and timber louvres. Exposed concrete construction is employed to moderate temperatures, using the 'air lake' principle of ventilation running beneath the buildings assisted by risers in each block. The surfaces beneath the building pre-cool the air, or warm it in the winter and then deflect it via wind towers to circulate

throughout the spine to the open air. Within the buildings the air is delivered via fans to provide cooling, with the electricity provided by photovoltaic panels.

The project exploits plan depth, sectional profile and orientation so that nature, climate and mass can compliment each other. The footprint of the buildings and courtyards is determined by the optimum layout for summer-time shading while maximising daylight penetration to teaching areas. A 'breathing skin' helps achieve passive downdraught evaporative cooling, providing with the other innovations a design where no energy input will be required for heating or cooling for 85 per cent of the year.[6] Openable windows maintain comfortable conditions in staff offices, seminar space and general teaching areas for most of the year, with mechanical systems employed only in the large lecture theatres.

Notes

1. *Student Energy Awareness Scheme – University of East Anglia,* Good Practice Case Study 367, DETR (Department of the Environment, Transport and the Regions), London (1998), p 3.
2. *Educated Energy – Good Housekeeping in Further and Higher Education Buildings,* Good Practice Guide 232, DETR (1998), sports facilities supplement.
3. Ibid, staff management supplement.
4. *Impact on the Region's Economy* (leaflet), Graduate School, California State University (1997), Chico, California.
5. *RIBA Journal,* September 1998, p 68.
6. *Architecture Today,* AT 90, July 1998, p 15.

Crime, politics and the university campus

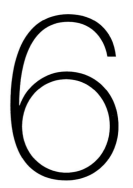

Crime on campus

The creation of a secure and safe learning environment is essential to the efficient functioning of a university. The existence of crime on campus undermines confidence students have in the management of university life. Crime is costly to universities in a number of ways – the replacement of equipment, the repair of buildings, poor recruitment of students and staff due to unfavourable image, and the additional cost of hiring private security firms.

The key to effective crime elimination is via a combination of design strategies and management policies. The campus masterplan and the design of individual buildings should seek to create an environment where crime opportunities are reduced to a minimum. The management and policing of the buildings and spaces should complement the design based crime prevention measures. Hence security issues should be incorporated early into design briefs, and police advice should be sought in the detailed development of the campus estate. However, there is a balance which needs to be struck between security and access. The democratic university is not a closed world of privileged scholars who enter via locked gates and use passwords at every door. Modern university education has at its core the provision of open access to knowledge and learning. Limits to movement should, therefore, be selective in time and space, and management policy in the crime prevention area should be discreet and understated.

The masterplan must establish a clear sense of unique territory for the university as a whole. It is important that the university is perceived as a special place: there needs to be character difference from the surrounding physical environment. This is not to establish exclusiveness, but to give identity to the place. Through identity comes a differentiation of space, edge and form which helps with crime management. It is important that those who visit the campus with criminal intent feel uncomfortable when they enter this special place. So the first principle is to avoid 'placelessness' in the making of the university.

6.1   The campus showing the importance of restricting entrance points and identifying territories.

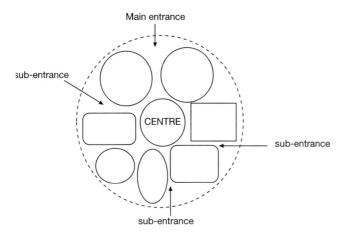

6.2   Surveillance from bay windows plus a clear definition of boundary give this block of student residences a feeling of security, Strathclyde University, Glasgow, UK.

The sense of territory relates to the whole but is equally true of the sub-territories and edges of faculty areas. Territoriality is best achieved by subtle means – a change of paving material, a low wall, a gateway building, a perimeter belt of tree planting. There may be actual gateways as well, especially at road entrances, but the perception of territory is an essential starting point for crime prevention.

Architectural design helps define territories. The walls of buildings contain and control space, they limit movement and direct flows. Hence, after the masterplan the next level of consideration is the design of individual buildings. Besides directing movement and providing opportunities for the surveillance of external and internal space, buildings also give definition to the sub-territories of a typical university (student village, science park, academic centre etc). At a more detailed level, buildings provide security and privacy. In the buildings themselves locked doors are essential for the safe storage of laboratory materials, equipment, staff records and examination papers. But not all buildings need to be locked at their entrance. Just as a progression of territory and security is needed on the campus as a whole, the same is true of individual buildings. There needs to be gradation from the perception of territory and security to real security by means of an escalating level of locking measures. Every building on campus should display the principles of crime prevention via territoriality, surveillance and physical locking.

6.3   These outdoor seats are well overlooked and help to provide surveillance at the building entrance. University of California, Berkeley, USA.

6.4 Hierarchy of crime prevention by design.

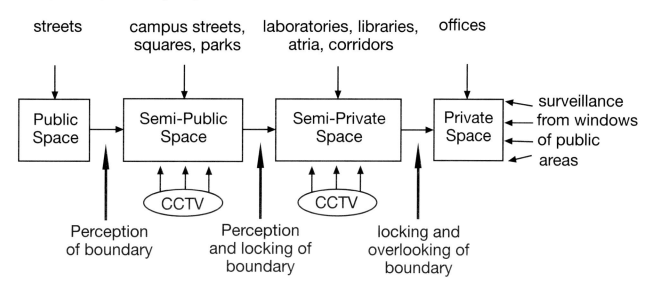

Surveillance is important so that the criminal is observed and feels that the observation is taking place. This means that external campus spaces and internal routes through buildings are overlooked by windows. In parallel there should also be surveillance cameras (CCTV) so that records are made of people on campus at the time of a crime. Again, the cameras should be seen not hidden: their value is psychological and real.

Managing crime prevention

There needs to be a correspondence between design-based crime prevention measures and management ones. According to a 1999 UK Home Office report on policing campuses, there is insufficient liaison between architectural measures and management policy for crime, and between academic and security staff at universities.[1] Most higher education institutions do not engage in an exchange of crime statistics between universities and local police authorities, neither are police officers actively encouraged onto campuses. Typically a university employs a private security firm or uses its own janitorial staff to double as campus policemen. As a consequence crime is not adequately addressed, neither are the necessary correspondences between physical design and crime management put in place.

Crime has an impact upon students, staff and visitors alike, and high levels of campus crime are a serious deterrent to recruitment. The Home Office advises that there should be greater liaison between public police

6.5 Well-peopled campus streets help to reduce crime.

authorities and private security firms on campus, especially in the field of data exchange and staff training.[2] The UK government encourages universities to make publicly available campus crime records including those at satellite sites such as halls of residence but few are willing to do so. Many do not publicise crime records, fearing an adverse impact upon morale and recruitment.

Most universities have a security strategy but only rarely does it influence campus planning or building design. It is this lack of correspondence which hampers long-term control of the problem. Many campuses in Europe and the USA face a major issue of drug and alcohol abuse. It is at the root of many subsequent problems such as car break-ins, attacks on people and equipment theft. Of the crimes on campus in the UK, burglary and theft are the most common (44 per cent) followed by vandalism (17 per cent), bicycle theft (13 per cent), theft from cars (9 per cent), theft of cars (5 per cent)[3]. Many thefts go unreported, such as those from student rooms or bags left unattended in libraries or lecture theatres, so about half of all campus crime is theft.

6.6 Campus policing at the University of Cape Town, South Africa.

6.7 Defining campus boundaries deters casual thieves, Stanford University, Palo Alto, USA.

There are five key principles to follow in making campuses safe and secure:

- design for crime prevention in masterplan and buildings
- liaison between university security staff and police authorities
- keep crime records, broken down into different sites and categories
- making crime records publicly available.
- providing close-circuit TV cameras (CCTV) in the most vulnerable areas.

Birmingham University: a case study of crime prevention

With a day-time population of thirty thousand, and a campus covering 120 hectares, Birmingham University crime records are lower than an equivalent urban area. This is attributed to the university employing fifty-four staff as security guards and a policy of direct collaboration between public policing and private campus policing. The university has a well-defined security strategy as part of the corporate planning process, and invests heavily in security because of its commitment to an 'investor in people' policy. The campus security plan subjects all areas of the university to surveillance from fixed or mobile security cameras, augmenting electronic coverage with twenty-four hour, all-

6.8 Well lit pedestrian routes at University of California, Berkeley, USA. Female students are particularly vulnerable to attack.

6.9 Well lit forecourts give a reassuring pretence to this library entrance. California State University, Chico, USA.

year-round, back up from police dogs and handlers.[4] The dogs were introduced at the request of students who complained of harassment at their halls of residence.

At Birmingham, as with other universities, the physical openness of the campus makes policing difficult. Although there are limits to vehicle penetration, the university is accessible to everybody on foot and the main university buildings such as the library and art gallery are also publicly available. The mission of the university and security are in many ways in conflict, yet effective policing has been achieved without creating a fortress environment. Cycle theft proved to be one of the biggest single areas of crime on campus and was overcome by a combination of CCTV installation, increasing security staff patrols of student cycle parking areas, and educating students into using tougher locks. This is typical of the approach at Birmingham University – physical changes, management changes and working with the student body.[5]

Computer theft was reduced by locking terminals to desks and introducing security tags to equipment but casual crime – bag theft, laptops, wallets – remains a problem. Opportunist crime undertaken by people casually walking through buildings is not easily controlled but again CCTV helps with subsequent identification of criminals. Although crime has diminished on campus, there are fears that it has been displaced to surrounding areas where street mugging is on the increase. However, since

Table 6.1 Crimes committed at Birmingham University Campus in 1998

Source: Birmingham University

many students are the victims of crime because of naivety, new students at Birmingham receive an information pack on crime protection measures plus a twice yearly *'Campus Watch'* magazine.

The campus as political protest

Whereas the university is generally regarded as a centre of intellectual life, the campus is also the arena for political protest. Many examples could be cited of the proponents of political change having used the lecture halls and streets of the university campus as the testing ground for fresh ideas. The University of Paris, for example, helped fan the fires of revolution which established the modern French state early in the nineteenth century. More recently anti-Vietnam war protest grew on the campuses of American universities before it broke out to engage the wider public. The unrest at Tiananmen Square, in 1989, began as a peaceful protest by students at the University of Beijing. At the time of writing students at the University of Tehran are engaged in an ideological battle with their government, again using the campus as the theatre of protest.

6.10 The campus is often the focus of political protest. Design can help ease conflict. University of Cape Town.

One reason for the predominance of the university campus in political protest is the tradition of openness and democracy which prevails in higher education. Another is the willingness often of chancellors and other senior academics to side with their students, thereby limiting the power of police to break-up demonstrations. This was the case, for instance, at Cape Town University where white students and academics alike openly challenged the apartheid movement in the 1970s. Here it transpired that the special powers of government security forces did not apply on South African campuses, thereby allowing them to become agents of change.

Quite how far the university masterplan should cater for student-led political protest is unclear. Certainly, the space for academic ceremonies and social discourse is also the space for political action. Students gather for many reasons on campus: academic, social, recreational and political. If the ideas generated in lectures and seminars are to have any benefit to society, they need to break free of the exclusive world of the university estate. The examples of political action mentioned earlier all led to student protest spilling out from the campus to the streets of the town. So one condition for peaceful student protest is to allow it to take place and then to provide a channel whereby it can spread further afield. The strategy should, therefore, be one of containment of space on campus with a well-defined corridor towards the centre of political power off campus. There are two benefits of this strategy, first, that the protests on campus can be contained and addressed by moderating forces, second, that the route off campus can be policed.

The politics of unrest on campus have to be considered at the masterplan stage. Students need to feel free to engage in political or social action, yet the destructive forces of agitation have to be controlled. Buildings and property should not be exposed to damage by poor design, neither should non-active students or staff feel threatened by such activity. Off campus too, political protest should be channelled and controlled so that its point can be made without bloodshed.

History teaches that the university campus is the focus for political and social challenges of various kinds. Many have been beneficial to society at large. How the balance of legitimate protest and law and order is maintained hinges partly upon the nature of space and connection generated in the arrangement of buildings and landscape on the campus.

Notes

1. Peter Kingston, 'Off the Record', *The Guardian Higher Education,* 27 April 1999, pp 1–2.
2. *Policing The Campus: Providing a Safe and Secure Environment*, Home Office, HMSO (1999), London.
3. Ibid.
4. Kingston, op cit p 2.
5. Ibid, and information provided by Birmingham University.

Part two

Buildings

CHAPTER

7

Libraries and learning resource centres

The university library is arguably the most important building on the campus. It is where the reservoir of knowledge and wisdom resides, making it a magnet for all members of the academic community. The library and its modern offshoot, the learning resource centre, requires a central location, prominent form, sheltered approaches, flexible internal accommodation, room for outward expansion, and a combination of open volume and private study space. Of all the buildings on the campus, the library defines the central area of the university by sheer bulk and symbolic significance.

The library is the signifier of learning in the way the lecture theatre signals teaching. Libraries are study centres, buildings where student-centred learning takes priority. Because of this they are rapidly evolving into computer-based learning resource centres where knowledge is held electronically, where interaction between scholars is via computer screens, where CD-Roms replace books, and where journals are retrieved through the touch of a keyboard. Irrespective of these changes in media, the library retains its central position in the environment of learning.

Over the centuries the university has played an important part in the development of the library as a distinctive

7.1 Doe Library, University of California, Berkeley, USA, by John G Howard (1911).

7.2 Library, University of East Anglia, Norwich, UK, by Denys Lasdun (1965).

modern building type. Because of their monastic or religious origins, universities became the custodians of early collections of books, developing in the process new ways of storing them and making printed material available to scholars. It was Trinity College library, Cambridge, which first introduced into UK academic libraries the European system of wall storage of books. The English had had a preference for the monastic stall system whereby books were chained to lecterns lit by a single window at right angles to the wall. Sir Christopher Wren at Trinity (1676), Nicholas Hawksmoor at All Souls, Oxford (1715), and James Gibbs at Radcliffe Camera, Oxford (1737), all used locked wall cases for the

storage of books with readers perched on free-standing desks in the aisle space. Domed libraries have long graced university campuses – their form being both symbolic and functional. Radcliffe Camera probably inspired Thomas Jefferson's domed library for the University of Virginia (1822) though Ètienne-Louis Boullée's unrealised designs published at the time may also have been influential. The idea found its way to two of America's finest academic libraries at the turn of the century – McKim, Mead & White's grand domed libraries for Columbia and New York universities.

7.3 Reading room, New York University, USA, library by McKim, Mead and White (1920).

Today many university libraries contain collections of national significance. Harvard University has a book collection approaching 10 million volumes, Berkeley 7 million, Yale 6 million and the Oxford and Cambridge libraries about 4 million. With such large numbers of books, let alone journals, the modern university library has had to separate storage from reading, and increasingly to use electronic means of scanning material. Added to this scholars now require copying facilities, access to personal computers, and the means of communicating electronically with other academics and other libraries. Some university libraries, in short, have become media centres with a book collection attached. Added to this the growth in student numbers has led to the evolution of the Learning Resources Centre, a form of library where the material is increasingly screen not book based; where videos, CD-Roms and the Internet replace the former

emphasis upon books and journals. To enter such buildings is to be confronted by computer terminals, not books, and by the hubbub of conversation or humming machines as against the silence of the traditional university library. The modern university library is, in fact, a market place of knowledge which students access at unprecedented speed.

The components of the library

Since books, journals and computer terminals represent the main means of accessing printed wisdom and knowledge, the university library consists of two main storage zones open to readers – the book and journal stacks, and the computer areas. Between the two is normally an entrance space, information and control points, lifts, stairs, display boards and offices for library staff. The segregation and zoning is vertical and horizontal, with open shelf storage areas as well as space for private reading, for group study, and for secure storage of material not normally on open shelves. In large libraries the storage areas often exceed those parts of the library open to scholars, and with particularly extensive or valuable collections, the storage of rare or infrequently used books may be at some distance from the library proper.

Modern university libraries usually provide study space for group work. Here silence is not enforced and occasionally tutorials or seminars may be conducted in designated areas. Since another trend is towards open planned, naturally ventilated libraries (often using a central atrium) a frequent problem is that of noise transfer to private study areas. The design and zoning of the library needs, therefore, to consider the management regime and how this may change with evolving theories of teaching and library-based learning.

A typical university with 20,000 students will have on open shelves some 3–500,000 books and 5–10,000 journals. In addition, there will be substantial storage, particularly for back copies of journals and periodicals. Large areas of storage are also needed for rarely used books and theses, making the total titles collection of a typical university about 1 million. Also current spending by universities is roughly equal between books and journals although science and research-based universities spend more on journals with

7.4 Library entrance, Temasek Polytechnic, Singapore, by Michael Wilford and Partners.

7.5 Satellite disks outside library at California State University, Sacramento, USA.

major growth (usually about 25 per cent of expenditure) on the acquisition of computer-based material. Books, journals, theses and electronic media require their own type of accommodation for browsing the material. While books are on open shelves in stacks normally placed at right angles to the perimeter wall, with about 1.2 metres of space between them, current journals are displayed face out on free-standing stacks with seating nearby; theses are in dedicated quiet areas sometimes with their own locked cabinets or secure accommodation. CD-Roms and other computer-based information material are generally located in computer suites with table-mounted PCs and work surfaces for transcribing from the screen to the notepad. As a rule of thumb in planning libraries 1 square metre of accommodation is allowed for every 40 volumes. This results in a library of 1 million books being about 25,000 square metres in area (eg California State University, Sacramento Library).

Two models are commonly found: either the integration of electronic media into the library, or the construction of separate accommodation for the digital information-cum-computer needs. In the first, books and computers share the library space with students moving freely between traditional and electronic sources. But three main disadvantages occur – the cost of cabling is high, equipment changes can be disruptive, and it is difficult to control the level of noise. With separate accommodation for electronic media normally known as Media or Learning Resource Centres the cost of cabling can be concentrated into a smaller area, a higher background noise level is accepted and upgrading of hardware or software does not disrupt the life of the library. However, separation discourages students from browsing (as against surfing) with the consequence that book and journal material is not so fully utilised. If libraries are to be effective in forging a total learning environment, then the decision regarding integration or separation is one which must relate to the mission of the university as a whole, especially its philosophy for teaching and learning.

Since many universities contain a central library and separate departmental libraries, there is the need to provide some of the above facilities in faculty buildings. Modern practice is, however, against localised libraries since they tend to be expensive to run, there is duplication of material, and students are not encouraged to explore books from outside their subject. However, departmental libraries do have the benefit of integrating lectures and seminars with written material within the faculty environment. Placing the main library catalogue and those in departments on a central computer system aids access to bibliographical and audio-visual material to all students, researchers and academics. Normally, departmental libraries operate the same access and loan regimes as the central library although in some areas, such as law, medicine or business studies, preference may be given to students from the department concerned.

At UC Berkeley there is the Doe Library (mainly postgraduate material), Moffitt Library (mainly undergraduate), Bancroft Library (rare and specialist material) and more than twenty branch libraries located in faculty buildings. Together they contain over 8 million volumes and countless maps, manuscripts and photographs. Many of the library's resources are duplicated in paper and electronic formats. Students at Berkeley are introduced to the various library resources via a single Information Centre which is responsible for updating the UC Berkeley Library web. This provides twenty-four-hour access to a variety of electronic databases including the *Encyclopaedia Britannica* and the images from the Louvre. Located on the first floor of the Moffitt Library is the Media Resources Centre which contains collections of video cassettes, audio cassettes, video disks, slides and a range of computer software programs. Hence, in spite of the size and complexity of provision, academics can access the library material via a variety of means and at times which suit them.

At Stanford University an even larger library, containing over 7 million books, 100 million archival manuscripts,

500,000 government documents, 1.5 million microform documents and 100,000 film items, is similarly split between main library, specialist libraries and departmental libraries. As with Berkeley, librarians spend much of their time instructing students in search and retrieval techniques, introducing them in their fresher year to Internet and web site facilities.

The main advantage of having a main central library and smaller specialised libraries elsewhere on campus is that the former can grow and change while the latter, where research and archival material is located, can remain fairly static. At Stanford the Green Library, progressively extended since 1891, contains the bulk of the book and journal collection. The upheavals here are in contrast to, for example, the Hoover Institution Library, founded in 1919 by Stanford alumni and US President Herbert Hoover, where the collection has grown in a more planned and gradual fashion.

Growth and change

Libraries pose a particular difficulty for universities. As they are required to acquire new material each year to keep the stock up to date, with the addition of perphaps twenty to fifty thousand new titles including journals they are perpetually growing in size. The difficulty is how to accommodate growth on this scale. Three answers are commonly adopted. First, to separate current books and journals from the storage of 'old' material using accommodation elsewhere on the campus for the purpose. Second, to maintain a critical mass of regularly used material, discarding older stock and relying upon inter-library loan or national collections for scarcely accessed titles. Third, to make increasing use of electronic media as against traditional books and journals, which is the approach of some of the 'new' universities in the UK. No solution to library growth is without accommodation or management problems, but it is clearly difficult to design a building which requires a possible 10 per cent increase in volume per year. This is based upon an assumption that book storage accounts for 25 per cent of total library area.

7.6 Concept sketch by Sir Norman Foster for the Law Library, University of Cambridge, UK.

Managing growth by the means above allows the university library to maintain coherence as a working entity. The problem arises when a university confronts some unexpected demand for change, such as the development of a whole new faculty, or if a collection of valuable archival material is lodged. In the first case the library will have to expand to provide space for the new study material. For academic reasons it is important that the new titles are integrated into the library collection with any fresh study space treated on equal terms with existing accommodation. The library should anticipate such growth at the outset, even if no foreseeable demand is in sight. In the second case, there is justification for a separate but related building constructed specifically to house the new material. Since it is likely to be a valuable collection there are security justifications for separation, and the scholars who use the material are often from outside the university. Integration of a special collection is not necessary, and there may be benefit in designing new buildings for such material in a distinctive fashion (eg Ruskin Library at the University of Lancaster, 1998).

All libraries are subject to incremental growth in material and the designer has to accommodate this at the outset. The best strategy is to provide some perimeter space for growth (both horizontally and vertically), to separate structural systems from enclosing elements (ie walls), to group service cores (lifts, stairs, ducts) on a rational evenly spaced basis, and to build to the highest standard of specification at the outset. This may cost more but provides greater long-term adaptive value. Flexibility is needed, especially in the different uses over time to which areas of the library can be put, in accommodating different security or control regimes, and in adapting to new forms of library media. It is possible to design a library with a high measure of flexibility but this is at the price sometimes of architectural quality (in the handling of space and light), and is expensive. The brief should establish the degree of adaptability required, and set reasonable standards bearing in mind other qualities to which a university library should aspire.

It is also important to consider the space needs of flexibility. If every part of the library is to be capable of any type

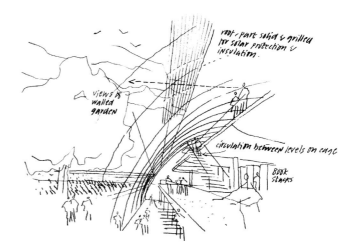

of use then air-conditioning is needed throughout. This is not only expensive and environmentally undesirable but is wasteful of space since air-conditioning requires a large amount of duct area. Rather than design for flexibility throughout it is better to consider the adaptability needs of specific zones. There are parts of the library, such as electronic media storage, which are expanding faster than others (for example/book storage) and the brief should identify the speed of change anticipated in different functional zones.

Space standards

A good rule of thumb is to allow 1 square metre per student when designing a university library. The allocation varies according to the type of university, the existence of separate faculty libraries, whether special collections exist, and the balance between electronic and traditional book-based material. Such are the different circumstances that a library can vary in size between 0.8 square metres and 1.2 square metres per student. So with a university of ten-thousand students a central library provisionally of 10,000 square metres is required. Of this area, it is assumed that a further space allowance is needed for corridors, stairs and toilets amounting to about 20 per cent of the initial area, making a total of 12,000 square metres for ten-thousand students.

Within the total space, specific accommodation is needed for:

- display on open shelves of books and periodicals
- storage of books and periodicals
- storage and use of audio-visual material
- display on tables of electronic media with supplementary storage
- catalogue search areas
- counter and control points
- copying facilities
- quick reference and short-loan area
- library offices
- seminar and tutorial rooms
- private study space (especially for postgraduates)
- small exhibition area.

Not all libraries will allocate the same amount of space to each element and some may dispense with certain categories of accommodation altogether. However, the typical university library will need a wider range of accommodation than a civic library because of the support needed for student-centred learning. This is particularly true in the area of electronic media where dedicated learning resource centres based on computer-based media are now the preferred form of library for science, technology, design and business-focused universities.

As a rule space in the library should be provided for readers' seats at a rate of 20 per cent of the student population. Where shelf browsing is replaced by screen scanning the percentage is higher, perhaps approaching 30–40 per cent in modern learning resource centres. Although the shelf and storage space demands of learning resource centres is lower than with traditional academic libraries, the extra seating area, table space and equipment costs of computer-based learning makes them generally more expensive to build and equip than traditional university libraries.

Of the total stock in a typical teaching-based university it is recommended that 70–80 per cent of books and periodicals should be on open access with the remainder on limited access. Storage needs are 8.4 metres per

7.7 Open access book shelves at Cranfield University library, Bedfordshire, UK, by Foster and Partners.

thousand volumes on open access and 4.2 metres per thousand for limited access material.[1] In many modern research-based universities the balance between open access and limited access material is 60 per cent to 40 per cent reflecting the importance of scientific journals or special collections.

In collegiate universities or in those universities with well established faculty libraries, there is a need to house some of the main stock and special collections at a local level. Typically a large college library may contain a hundred thousand books and subscribe to maybe one thousand periodicals. Generally, the higher the standard of course provided the greater is the demand made upon library space. Those universities with a large number of masters programmes and with plenty of research students (let alone research active staff) require more library space, more books and journals, and more plentiful access to computer-based study support than other universities. Hence guidelines of space and book provision are subject to modification when the library context is examined. In fact, the UK Department of Education and Science recommends that space allowances can be varied by 30 per cent depending upon degree level.[2]

Normally, the designer seeks to provide a library which is heavily used since this suggests a good utilisation of resources. Under-used libraries are indicative of poor design, excessive space provision, and duplication between central and faculty provision. Heavy use, however, should provide space also for quiet study, for reflecting on the material available, and for intensive periods of writing. Hence a university library needs to zone noisy from quiet areas, open spaces from small study areas, and set aside rooms for group work. With so much computer-based library material now available, the importance of silent working space should not be underestimated.

Space standards are advisory and university librarians tend to have their own ideas about the nature, character and level of provision needed in any particular library. However, published standards are:

- one reader space for every four to five students based upon 2.5 square metres per reader
- 1 square metre of shelf-based storage space for every hundred books (one book/volume = .01 square metres of library space)
- library office space is 12 per cent of total library space
- circulation areas represent about 25 per cent of total library space
- eight to ten books per square foot in open-shelf reading room, ten to twelve in open stack, twelve to fifteen in closed stack, and fifty to sixty in compact storage.[3]

Technical factors

There are several factors to consider which make the university library almost unique among campus buildings in the complexity of technical requirements. The main issues are noise, humidity, structural loading, glare and computer cabling.

Noise There is the general expectation that since libraries are quiet places external noise will be suppressed by good design of the building fabric, and internal noise abated by the sound choice of partitions, carpets and air-conditioning systems. Where external noise is a problem then the library may have to employ a sealed, double-glazed building envelope with full air-conditioning. Normally, however, a library can be at least partially ventilated with opening windows either to the outside world or to internal atria as at Queen's Building, Anglia Polytechnic University.

7.8 The environment of the library should maximise natural light, views and interconnection. Cranfield University library, Bedfordshire, UK, by Foster and Partners.

Internal noise is a greater problem, especially with the growth in student-centred learning which is a feature of many 'new' universities. The best strategy is to zone the library into degrees of quietness using glazed partitions or bookstacks to achieve sound separation. Carpets may be needed in potentially noisy areas but are inappropriate in heavily used parts of the library such as around the control points. Acoustic tiles may be needed especially in the domed reading rooms of older academic libraries.

Sound absorbing finishes are often required in the reading or browsing areas of libraries. Although the books themselves prevent sound reflection to a degree, the design of surfaces (walls, floors, ceilings) and the use of soft furniture have a part to play in creating a quiet environment. Air-conditioning with its quiet hum can help suppress sharp noises.

Open-plan libraries pose a particular difficulty and here the level of noise acceptance is often higher than in the traditional university library. The main types of noise which require to be suppressed are conversation, keyboard-tapping sounds and electronic buzzes, and fabric transmitted noise such as lift doors or footsteps on stairs. Different strategies are required for each type of noise, and different levels of tolerance required for separate zones of the library. As a rule the maximum internal noise level should be 45–50dB but much depends upon cultural factors and the relationship between aural and visual distraction.

7.9 Section, Law Library, University of Cambridge, UK. Norman Foster and Partners.

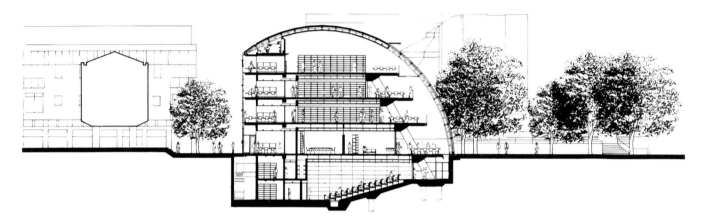

Humidity Books, journals and electronic media require a well-tempered environment. Where there is too much water vapour present in the atmosphere the paper-based materials may suffer from mould or mite attack, where there is too little the paper may dry out. As a result where rare or antiquarian books, prints or drawings are held, the question of relative humidity is an important one.

Moist air may be introduced into the library either through external windows or as a by-product of the number of readers present. Humidity is not only a problem for the conservation of books but leads to fabric condensation which can give rise to rust stains (as on shelving systems) and moisture transmission through ducts. The recommended humidity level in libraries is about 50 per cent and slightly higher with full air-conditioning. However in IT-based libraries the humidity level is usually slightly lower (around 45 per cent) in order to avoid moisture contamination of disks and computer terminals.

Structural loading The weight of books and their concentration into stacks means that libraries are subject to heavy point loads. Books weigh about 16 kilogrammes per metre shelf run and bound periodicals about 27 kilogrammes. A typical library needs to be able to support imposed loads of books of 1.2–2.6 kN/m^2 throughout the stack areas.[4] With compact shelving systems such as those used in book stores the loads may be considerably higher. Taken together with other imposed loads (people, furniture, book-shelving systems) means that the structure needs to be capable of distributing, according to the UK University Grants Committee recommendation, a loading of 6.3–7.0 kN/m^2.[5]

The weight of the library material adds considerably to the cost of the building in terms of the thickness of floors, size of columns and beams, and depth of foundations. If total operational flexibility is required then all areas will have to be constructed to the same high structural standards. Realistically, limits have to be set upon internal change, and loading levels vary for offices (5 kN/m^2), reading rooms (6 kN/m^2), open-stack (7 kN/m^2), compact stack storage areas (10 kN/m^2). The typical electronic media library is subject to less loading pressure and can be designed with an imposed level of 5–6 kN/m^2.

Glare and lighting From an environmental and cost point of view it is important to maximise the use of natural light. However, direct sunlight needs to be controlled in order to avoid excessive solar heat gain and to eliminate glare. Direct sunlight, and daylight in certain circumstances, can damage certain papers, vellum and parchment, and lighting control is needed particularly where special collections of books or drawings exist. Daylight needs to be controlled too in the vicinity of computer screens in order to avoid discomfort and eye strain.

Natural light carries advantages in terms of the cost of running the library, displays good environmental behaviour and creates a lively and satisfying interior for readers. Daylight is available via perimeter glazing, roof lighting and the use of internal glazed courts. To maximise the use of natural light the library should have a plan depth of no more than 15 metres between perimeter light sources (ie outside or via atria), and where light is only available from one side the depth of daylight penetration restricts the room to 7–8 metres. The efficiency of light penetration into the library via windows can be enhanced by the use of light shelves, the splaying of window surrounds and by employing light-coloured reflective surfaces. However, windows lead to heat loss in the winter, heat gain in the summer, pose security threats to the library collection, and can lead to glare in readers' eyes if not well designed. The advantages of perimeter glazing, however, should not be overlooked: peopled facades lead to lively buildings and reduced crime because of the surveillance provided.

Heat loss and gain can be controlled by the type, thickness and depth of glass as well as the use of external or internal blinds on southern faces. Glare, however, is less easily controlled since it is subject to two variable conditions – the angle and intensity of the sun and the sensitivity of the reader. Glare is the result of direct sunlight entering the eye and in order to reduce glare sunlight needs to be deflected from as many sources as possible before it reaches the reader. The ideal working environment in a library is one of even gradation of light from the source (natural or artificial) to the book and table top. The ratio of luminance between window and wall (or light source and shade with artificial light), wall and ceiling or floor, ceiling and table top, and finally table top and book should reduce in a proportion of about three to one at each stage. The aim should be to provide a lighting level of at least 400 lux in reading areas, 600 lux in the counter and control areas, 200 lux in open stack areas, and 100 lux in closed book stores.[6]

Computer cabling The impact of computer-based information systems fundamentally effects space use in the traditional university library. The new IT-based knowledge systems form the hub not only of the central library but the whole campus masterplan. The network of IT systems, which may be centrally located in the Learning Resource Centre, extends outwards across campus in the form of audio-visual work stations and networked reader desks in faculty libraries or departmental offices and study bedrooms. Information retrieval is often through links to other national or academic institutions and via satellite connections to global sources. These advances in information technology alter the pattern of learning, aiding the development of distance learning packages and destroying traditional spatial relationships. The growth too in twenty-four-hour operations, in CCTV studios for learning, and teaching packages on home TV and via the Internet, all directly or by implication alter the assumptions upon which the library has evolved. The computer destroys distance, making virtual worlds that can erode the very concept of what constitutes a library.

The use of electronic media of various kinds means the academic library today is a different animal to that in operation a decade ago. The modern library has to provide access to the rapidly expanding world of educational videos, CD-Roms, electronic catalogues and the Internet while giving students their own computer workstations capable of sending e-mails, printing reports and down-loading electronic data onto screen or in paper format. Books and journals are still needed but increasingly the material they contain is summarised on CD-Rom with key points accessed electronically via digital formats.

The new universities in the UK (those established in 1992 from former polytechnics), community colleges in the USA and the freshly established universities in Asia are leading the change from paper-based to electronic information library systems. The resulting pressures are twofold: first, to evolve a new typology for the computer-focused university library (usually known as a Learning Resource Centre) and second, to adapt older academic libraries to the new technologies. With the growth in electronic computer-based media, teaching and learning strategies have had to change, and this creates a momentum for space redistribution in older libraries. New libraries are becoming electronic media centres, often directly linked to university computer departments and open twenty-four hours a day. In such buildings word processing replaces the traditional emphasis upon book browsing. Since CD-Roms cannot readily be borrowed, the Learning Resource Centre is more intensively occupied than the older style library.

The number of workstations available dictates the cabling needs but since the growth in computers is exceeding most other areas of library investment, some over-capacity is needed if future demand is to be met. The world of computer-based learning is evolving rapidly and flexibility is essential. This is normally achieved by employing multi-point perimeter cabling (with traditional as well as fibre-optic systems) throughout the library (except in utility and storage areas) with raised floor ducting in the most intensively used areas.

7.10a   Section, computer-based library, University of Sunderland, UK, by Building Design Partnership.

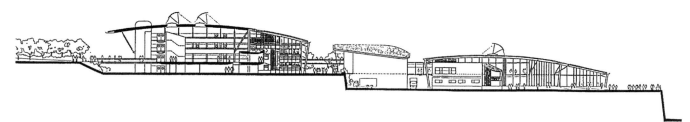

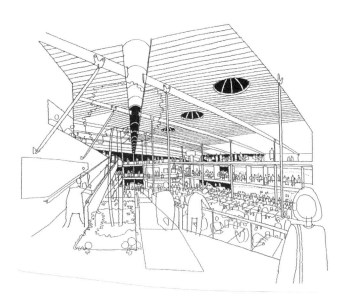

7.10b   (Left) Concept sketch.

7.10c   (Bottom Left) Site plan.

Since the life of computer equipment, both hardware and software, is fairly short, the astute librarian will invest in cabling flexibility. This maximises choice and avoids disruption to the workings of the library in the future. One trend is that since computers are becoming smaller, cheaper, yet more efficient and with greater power, their use is now commonplace for nearly all students whether studying music or physics. The level of provision of personal computer workstations in university libraries varies greatly between one in fifty of the student population to one in six in some recently built new universities in the UK (eg University of Sunderland). In some ways the use of Information Technology symbolises new knowledge and distinguishes new from old universities. For those campuses in the inner city the specialist computer study and training facilities reflected by the learning resource centre mirrors the changing pattern of work in society at large.

The widespread use of IT systems in academic libraries has encouraged the emergence of the library as a training centre for computer skills. The modern library is not merely a place where information is accessed but part of the learning environment of the university. As a consequence there are seminar rooms and lecture theatres adjacent to the computer suites where students can be trained in using the equipment and encouraged to develop new skills. The library is part of the development of computer literacy; cabling needs to take account of training requirements as well as traditional library ones.

Two Case Studies of Modern Libraries

(a)   *Paul Hamlyn Learning Resource Centre, Thames Valley University, Slough, UK*

This building breaks the mould of the university library by placing the emphasis upon space and computer-based access, rather than on books and shelves.

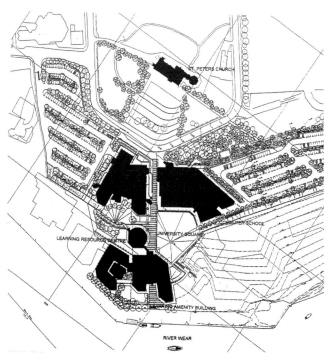

7.11 Entrance, Learning Resource Centre, Sheffield Hallam University, UK, by FaulknerBrown Architects.

7.12 Layout diagram for unversity library.

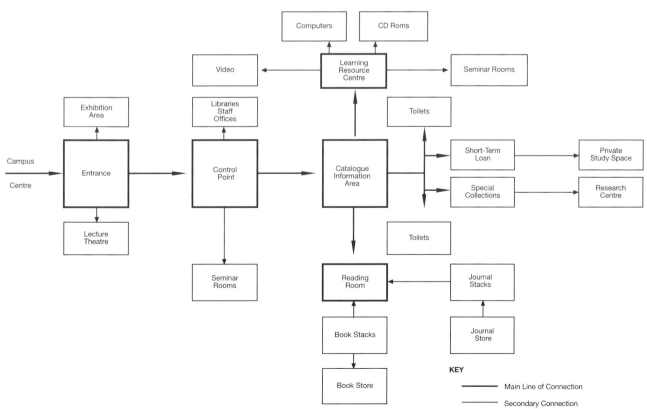

Table 7.1 Typical PC-based information services in electronic library

Access to selected BIDS databases
CD-Rom network
British Library Catalogue
Library Catalogue
Netscape (access to Internet)
Word
Excel
Powerpoint

Source: University of Huddersfield, 1998

It is a barn-like building with the expansiveness of an aircraft hangar and the cool neutral lighting of a modern high-tech factory. Designed by the Richard Rogers Partnership in 1995, the Paul Hamlyn Learning Resource Centre in Slough, west of London, aims to provide an exciting and flexible space in which students can, as the vice-chancellor put it, 'study at their own pace, in their own time, using a variety of learning styles'.[7]

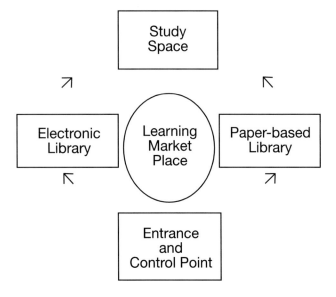

7.13 Conceptual diagram for modern university library.

The building is designed to be the electronic hub of the university with networked links to local colleges, business and the global community. To make the IT element visible and accessible the computer terminals are located in a massive open-planned entrance foyer. Here, with a three-storey wall of book stores acting as an environmental moderator to the west side, students can sit in front of their screens while watching the world go by in a space which uplifts the spirit and encourages sociability. Learning is not seen at Thames Valley University as a private and competitive endeavour but one where team working is important and where social and academic discourse interact. The building is designed to express this style of learning, and, being central to the philosophy of pedagogy at Thames Valley, it is naturally located at an important cross-roads of student movement at the heart of the campus.

The Learning Resource Centre is simple in plan: a three-storey wing of book stacks provides a buttress to the steel and glass arch which contains the electronic library. The two are linked by an open gallery with lightweight bridges – themselves a metaphor for the delicate nature of the connection between the traditional and digital library. The gables of the arched section are clear glazed to facilitate views in and out. At night the building is a beacon of learning with students and staff going about their business bathed in highly visible light. Without walls or columns to impede sight lines the building is the kind of open, interactive trading floor adapted to the ethos of the new universities.

The bold shapes and primary colours send out a message of confidence. Visitors to the campus are in no doubt about the function of the building – its inner workings are forever visible and the pattern of newly formed pedestrian spaces signals the importance of this campus building. The immediate landscape has been refashioned to focus upon the Learning Resource Centre with Rogers himself responsible for the choice of site and the adaptations required of the masterplan. Tree planting is an important complementing element

7.14 Perspective view, Paul Hamlyn Learning Resource Centre, Thames Valley University, Slough, UK, by Richard Rogers Partnership.

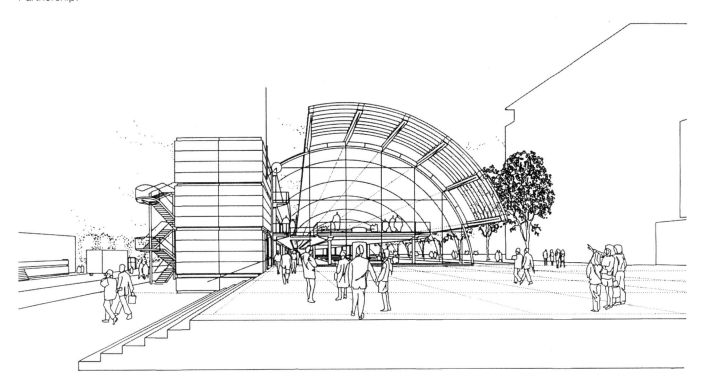

of the design: a line of specimen trees establishes a powerful north–south axis across the campus, anchored at one end by the Learning Resource Centre. The trees guide visitors to the building, provide shade from the morning sun, help locate the geometry of the new pool provided alongside the Learning Resource Centre, and give a point of interest to views out of the library windows.

The large volume of the computer hall and the thermal capacity of the bookstack are the key environmental factors obviating the need for air conditioning. The building is naturally lit and ventilated with air taken in across the outside pool and released via high level vents in the roof space between arch and the rectangular bookstack block. Computer-generated heat and body heat play an important role in the low-energy strategy, helping to achieve the relative efficient energy level of 100 kWhrs/m^2 at peak occupancy.[8] In this sense the learning and environmental strategies are both addressing future agendas in a self-supporting fashion.

(b) Ruskin Library, University of Lancaster, UK

The Ruskin Library (1998) is a special collection of study material containing books, paintings and letters, devoted to the life and work of the great nineteenth-century critic John Ruskin. It is the largest

Building	Architect	Special Features	Cost
Paul Hamlyn Learning Resource Centre, Thames Valley University	Richard Rogers Partnership	• Transparency removes barriers to learning • Library which is mainly electronic • Deliberate fashioning of image to reflect creative flair. • Low-energy strategy based upon natural ventilation	£1,013/m^2 (in 1996)

single archive on Ruskin, and was put together by Howard Whitehouse MP over a period between 1910–55. The collection was moved from the South of England to Lancaster to be closer to other Ruskin collections, such as that held in Cumbria at Brantwood House on Lake Coniston where Ruskin lived for many years.

The new library makes reference to Ruskin, to the surrounding landscape, and to the immediate environs of the University of Lancaster. By addressing all three the building becomes immediately a structure of complexity with different nuances appealing to visitors with quite different expectations. As a special collection the plan has a tomb-like quality with thick curved walls enclosing in their embrace the precious collection. The oval form of the building is split on the long axis to let the sunlight in and to open the interior to views across the landscape towards Lake Coniston. Just as Ruskin's ideas shed light upon the Victorian world, so too this building, designed by MacCormac Jamieson Prichard, plays upon the metaphor of darkness and light.

7.15 Entrance, Ruskin Library, University of Lancaster, UK, by MacCormac, Jamieson Prichard.

From the point of view of the campus, created originally to plans by Shepheard Epstein in 1965, the Ruskin Library forms a new gateway building. Positioned astride the road which takes visitors into the university, the keep-like shape is both landmark and deflector of sightlines to the northern and southern campus. Here the curved walls do not just contain the collection, they allow the eye to be taken to points further afield – groups of trees, the main academic library and mountains beyond.

The building is not only an external landmark, it creates an atmospheric experience based upon the notions of Ruskin by the skilful manipulation of plan, section and construction materials. The plan, both contained and prized open on the dominant east–west axis, has a central suite of offices and meeting rooms reached by passageways and bridges with glazed floors. Stairs following the curving line of the perimeter wall make contact with the concrete of the interior casket-like galleries which is stained black to recall slate. The glass panels in the floor allow light and views to filter up and down, dematerialising the normal sense of construction surface.

In section the distinction between archival storage on lower floors and gallery-cum-library spaces above is equally ambiguous yet visually stimulating. The archive section is a building within a bigger building – a kind of Russian doll effect of layers of ever greater complexity. These effects, which draw in part upon Ruskin's thesis in *The Seven Lamps of Architecture* (1848), give animation and character to the facades. The bands of stone, glass and textured concrete do not directly reflect internal functions but recall Ruskin's admiration for polychrome construction. The facade and interior have two quite different agendas and each is developed against principles of their own. Ruskin was a complex and intriguing figure whose nature this building captures with style and sophistication.

Users of the library normally pre-arrange for the study material to be made available. In this sense the building is unusual, almost exclusive and certainly

7.16   Ruskin Library, University of Lancaster, UK, by MacCormac, Jamieson Prichard.

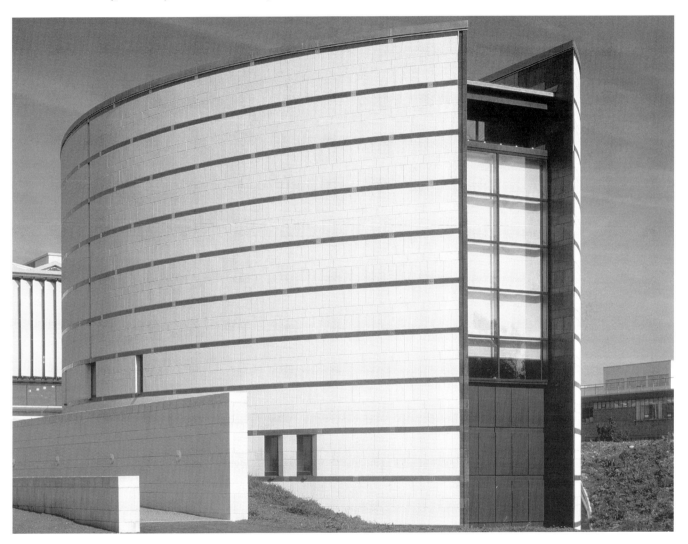

redolent with potential scholarship. The study spaces are not neutral but are bedecked in references to Ruskin, not only in the objects and bric-à-brac of his life on display, but in the modern furniture designed with regard to Ruskin's ideals. The tables and chairs constructed by 'honest workmen using the best English material' – in this case oak, walnut and red-stained leather – stand like sculpture in the space, giving aesthetic intensity to the building.

The building also explores one further dimension of Ruskin's legacy – that of environmental design. In this building a moat follows the line of the perimeter walls acting as a source of pre-cooled air in order to obviate the use of air-conditioning.[9] This building is the first passively conditioned archival library in the UK. The thick perimeter walls, large internal volume and inter-connectedness of the spaces inside all provide the means to exploit new approaches to library design.

Building	Architect	Special Features	Cost
Ruskin Library, University of Lancaster	MacCormac Jamieson Prichard	• Archive library for Ruskin collection • Acts as landmark and gateway to campus • Innovative environmental design • Interior character based upon Ruskin ideals	£4.5 million

Notes

1. Godfrey Thompson, *Planning and Design of Library Buildings* (Third Edition), Butterworth Heinemann (1989), Oxford, p 208.
2. Ibid, p 209.
3. Data based upon various summaries in G Thompson, op cit. Thompson quotes sources in UK, USA and New Zealand.
4. Ibid, p 73.
5. See *The Architects' Journal,* 21 February 1968, p 459, for further details.
6. Summarised from Illuminating Engineering Standards (IES), *Lighting Handbook* (1981) and G Thompson op cit.
7. *The Architects' Journal,* 10 October 1996, p 30.
8. Ibid, p 34.
9. Peter Davey, 'The Eighth Lamp' *The Architectural Review,* June 1998, p 68.

Laboratories and research buildings

CHAPTER

8

Research laboratories are an essential component of the modern university campus. Without research the university will quickly lose its cutting edge in teaching as well as its reputation as a centre of higher education. Research and teaching are inexorably entwined even in non-science-based universities. To the university research has three main benefits – the enrichment of teaching, reputation enhancement and income generation. To fulfil these three primary roles the university requires well-equipped and suitably designed laboratories. Investment in the infrastructure of research, although expensive, carries long-term advantages for the university.

8.1 Mudd Chemistry Building (left), Gilbert Bioscience Building (right) by Arthur Erickson Associates at Stanford University, Palo Alto, USA.

8.2 The key role of laboratories.

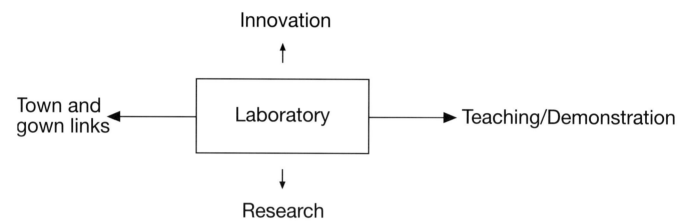

Laboratories come in many forms depending largely upon the subject catered for. Whereas laboratories have their basis mainly in testing and research, they are also used widely in teaching. In many universities laboratories are also high-tech corridors, facilitating a transfer of ideas and cultures between industry and academia. They are for the student one of the closest experiences while at university of the world of work and of directly applying research methodologies.

For these reasons the laboratory should be seen as a symbolic gateway of learning – the place where teaching ceases and research begins. The laboratory should not, therefore, be tucked away off campus or located in an exclusive research enclave at the periphery of the university. The laboratory needs to be more centrally positioned so that the links between teaching and research can be developed while at the same time providing ease of access for researchers, some of whom may not be university staff in the traditional sense. Also since much research involves industry or business partnership, the laboratory provides a useful mechanism for facilitating town and gown links. The design of laboratories needs to reflect therefore the academic aspirations of the university as well as the specific demands of the research environment.

While laboratories come in many forms depending upon the needs of specific faculties (medical, engineering science, biological science etc) they can be classified in terms of the balance between pure research, applied research, demonstration and teaching. In most modern university laboratories there is an element of demonstration and teaching. How these are accommodated within the envelop of research depends upon the balance of teaching and research, the health and safety implications, and of the type of research undertaken.

Laboratory buildings nearly always have a rational plan whose characteristics sometimes reflect the organisation or geometry of their subject. Discipline in plan and section, order in room layout, operational flexibility and extendibility are the essential features of laboratories. Rational planning leads to modular or prefabricated methods of construction with building services readily accessible to facilitate periodic upgrading. Since research is a fast growing activity, room or laboratory layout needs to be unencumbered by the permanence of walls or partitions. For these reasons most laboratories employ wide-span structures so that columns do not impede flexibility. Consequently many laboratories are single storey and roof-lit to allow for good light distribution. Deep roof spaces are generally used to house mechanical services with or without suspended ceilings.

Until recently laboratory design varied between one type of facility and another. The needs of different subjects shaped laboratories into different forms. However, current practice is to provide research space devoid of subject characteristics. This gives the university greater operational flexibility and by employing modular construction with limited planning variety, it helps keep down costs. Modularity too helps with

8.3 William Gates Computer Science Building, Stanford University, Palo Alto, USA, by Robert Stern.

8.4 Axonometric, Engineering Building, Leicester University, UK, by James Stirling. The design distinguishes between research, administration and teaching.

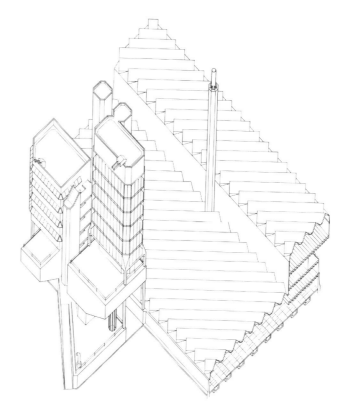

replacing damaged parts since the university can keep a supply of materials knowing that at some point they will be needed. Design, procurement, construction and maintenance are held in close cycles of dependence in laboratory buildings.

Unlike private research centres, the university research laboratory normally caters for undergraduate as well as research students. Most science-based undergraduate degrees now contain an element of applied research. There is the expectation that first degree graduates will be conversant with research methods and familiar with research equipment. Handling students in laboratories puts particular pressure upon health and safety especially when accommodating different levels of students. Since most university laboratories are used for research, demonstration and teaching, the space sequences and equipment areas need to be able to cater for diverse functions. The flow of groups of undergraduates between demonstration classes has a different characteristic to the more singular movement of individual researchers.

The culture of science and technology, which the modern university expresses and helps to fashion through research, places an obligation on laboratory buildings to be 'intelligent buildings' themselves. Research buildings not only need to be 'knowledgeable' but to facilitate the expansion of knowledge in their fields. An intelligent building is one

which uses the latest technology (mainly computerised systems) to control the internal environment so that there is a healthy, secure, comfortable and productive laboratory environment. Good environmental design and sensible use of fabric sensors allows the building to perform well and adapt over time.

Computers are at the centre of most university laboratories. Computers are used to control experiments, to record results, to analyse the findings, and to explain graphically the experimental patterns. The laboratory has, therefore, three main systems to integrate – the research environment, that of demonstration and the computer network. The research environment will probably consist of various types of facility to allow experiments to take place (testing rigs, electron microscopes, laser measurement etc). Demonstration will require tables, projection equipment, large screen television, display space for models and the like. The computer network will consist of workstations, printers and disk storage plus fibre-optic cabling. These three systems converge in the typical university laboratory, they share space and personnel but they also have their own operational demands. Certain testing equipment, for instance, poses a serious risk to health while computers have a short lifespan especially in the knowledge intensive research areas. Security, replacement and physical separation are needed but to be an effective part of the university's

learning environment, the three main systems need to overlap and integrate.

Surveillance is needed to protect staff and equipment. Some research undertaken in universities raises difficult ethical issues, such as defence work or animal experimentation, and in other areas where new drugs or ideas are being developed there needs to be intellectual security until the work is patented. Since research can contribute up to one half of a university's funding, although normally the level is around 20–30 per cent, the sensitivity of the work is high. In research areas which are externally funded, the sponsoring organisation has a vested interest in exploiting the results before others can do so. Researchers have an understandable interest to ensure their intellectual copyright is not abused. Privacy and security are an inevitable component of the generation of research ideas. Once the material is published or patented it is, of course, available to all to exploit, but until that time the research lab needs to be secure.

Electronic surveillance is a feature of most university laboratories, even those which are used significantly for teaching purposes. Such surveillance gives extra security to equipment (especially computers) and to staff and students. Radioactive material is commonly used in experimentation, and some materials used in the development of drugs are toxic; even when substances are inert, with combustion they can become highly poisonous. Hence, most modern laboratories have sophisticated systems for recording the movement of people or materials through the building in general and especially into the most sensitive areas. Vandalism, espionage and burglary are all effectively reduced by CCTV and various other forms of electronic surveillance.

Laboratories consist of large science-based spaces where heat gain is a problem and small ancillary areas (offices) which often require heating. The functional, structural and environmental strategy can be brought to work together by, for example, using an exposed concrete frame to absorb heat in the lab area, and by utilising a lightweight steel frame in the office and ancillary areas. The concrete frame absorbs day-time heat and releases it slowly overnight whereas the steel frame and lightweight panels of office areas can respond quickly to different needs. Hence the 'served' spaces (lab-

8.5 Research often entails the use of hazardous materials. Gas storage, Stanford University, Palo Alto, USA.

8.6 Concept sketch (above) and laboratory layout (below) at the Institute of Biomedical Sciences Building, University of Strathclyde, Glasgow, UK, by Reiach and Hall.

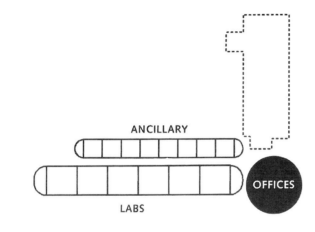

ORGANISATIONAL CONCEPT

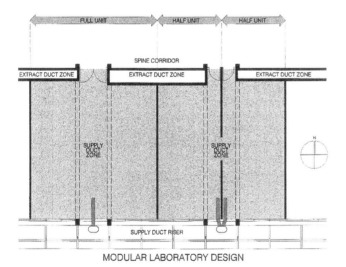

MODULAR LABORATORY DESIGN

oratories) and 'servant' spaces (offices) have different structural forms bred of both functional and environmental dictates. It is an approach evident at the Institute of Biological Sciences Building at the University of Strathclyde (1995) designed by Reiach and Hall. Here a clear distinction is made between laboratory, ancillary, social and office areas, each having their own structural grid and method of construction. In the south-facing laboratories a structural bay 9.6 x 10.8 metres is employed, bisected by a supply duct zone linked to perimeter extract duct zones. Across the corridor a smaller structural width is employed for the ancillary accommodation constructed of steel as opposed to the concrete of the labs. The effect is to moderate temperatures by constructional means, to give the building visual variety between spaces and facades, and to reflect operational requirement in the different structural grids employed.[1]

The laboratory is one aspect of a crucial three-way relationship within the learning environment of a university. The library, lecture theatre and laboratory each represent a different aspect of intellectual development. The library is to learning what the lecture theatre is to teaching, and the laboratory is to research. Consequently, the university laboratory does not normally have its own library, although it will need access via campus web sites to library material, or an integral lecture theatre. Only at the level of demonstration does teaching play a large part in the lab. Figure 8.8 is a useful conceptual diagram but it also suggests a spatial relationship for the layout of the campus. The three elements do not have equal status across universities or within a single university. At Cambridge University, for instance, research facilities are conspicuous, even in places dwarfing the college libraries and halls of residence. Conversely, at the new campus of the University of Lincolnshire and Humberside, the library dominates. Formal or spatial supremacy needs to reflect the mission and characteristics of the university.

The inventions discovered by researchers in universities find their way eventually to new theories promulgated via the curriculum. In this sense, although teaching prepares stu-

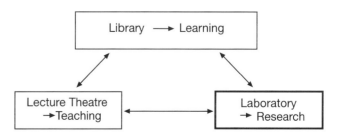

8.7 Conceptual diagram of linkage of intellectual development at a typical university.

dents for the world of applied research, the research undertaken drives the flow of new knowledge from universities to industry. It is difficult to envisage a world without university-based research – either basic or applied. There would be no penicillin, atomic power, computers, photovoltaics, organ transplants or bioengineering. These discoveries did not always originate in a single university or a university working in isolation from experts in industry. Most discoveries are the result of research partnership between academics, private research centres and industry. The laboratory, with its research facilities, staff areas, meeting and seminar rooms must create an environment of co-operation, exploiting the serendipity of chance discovery. While for practical purposes rationality must pervade the plan, there should be sufficient contact with beauty and nature to provide the environment necessary for reflection. Without quiet contemplation and accidental encounter with other researchers, originality may become stifled.

Many research centres have an island of reflection at their centre – a kind of oasis of trees, water and flowers cut off from the wider world. This may exist as an internal atrium within the body of the laboratory complex, or as an external garden. Alternatively, the research centre can be located in a landscape park with the individual laboratories designed as transparent pavilions in close contact with nature. This is the approach at the Science and Engineering Quad at Stanford University masterplanned by I M Pei in 1994.

Social interaction is a key element of laboratory design. The fabric of the building should encourage chance encounter not discourage it by, as commonly occurs, excessive enclosure or security. Modern surveillance can provide effective security without walls, and space, which

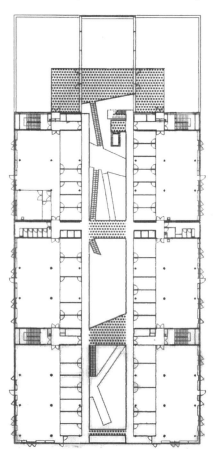

8.8   Interior visualisation, Centre for Clinical Research Sciences, Stanford University, Palo Alto, USA, by Foster and Partners.

8.9   Plan, Research Centre, University of Marne-La-Vallée, Paris, France, by Jourda and Perraudin.

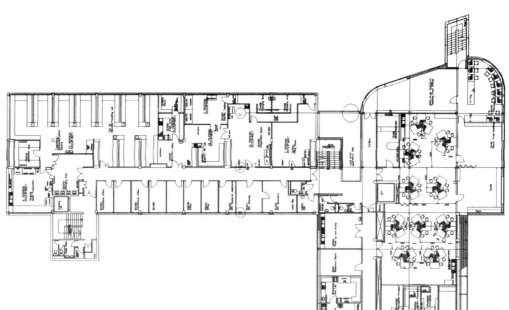

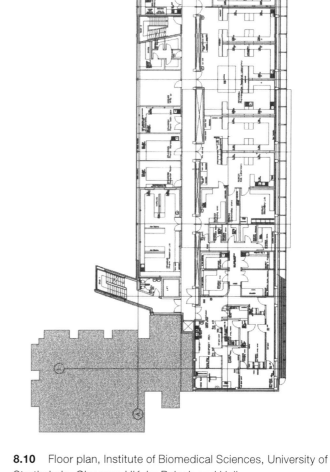

is the medium of social interaction, should not be solely directed towards functional activities. Interaction occurs at key points in the laboratory: at the building entrance, along corridors and in community or shared areas. The latter should be generous but with 'dens' to facilitate semi-private team discussion. There needs to be space for all: territory for groups and quiet areas for individuals. In this sense the laboratory is not abstract zoned space but a research environment where originality, invention, innovation and insight are encouraged by careful design.

Detailed design of laboratories

In the teaching university, laboratories are not usually designed to serve specific research needs. Instead they are arranged as flexible spaces able to cater for different academic subjects. Only in larger universities where medical schools or advanced research takes place are laboratories tailored to subject needs. It is a characteristic of modern universities that knowledge and research priorities evolve rapidly over time. Laboratories, therefore, need to facilitate change in the management of research, in the provision of research equipment, and in the nature of the research undertaken. Only in the most advanced research universities is it common to find specialised laboratory facilities.

How flexibility is achieved varies between types of laboratory. However, as a general rule large uninterrupted volumes are the norm with the services required to undertake research kept apart from structural members and positioned so that they are readily accessible and replaceable. Into these volumes different kinds of equipment-benching, gases and security can be provided, each with their own lifetimes of use. In fact, the building should be divided between working bays and service bays in plan, and

8.10 Floor plan, Institute of Biomedical Sciences, University of Strathclyde, Glasgow, UK, by Reiach and Hall.

in more elaborate laboratories in section as well. The dimension of the bays depends upon circumstance but is normally 7–10 metres wide for working bay and 2–3 metres wide for a service bay. Room heights are usually 3–4 metres but can be less with suspended ceilings. In multi-storey laboratories there may be intermediate service floors, or alternatively a sub-basement or roof service floor. In large single-storey laboratories basement servicing with underfloor access for vehicles tends to be preferred.

Laboratories require three main types of accommodation: the research laboratories themselves, small teaching and seminar rooms, and offices. Research staff need accommodation near to the labs while facility managers and professors require private offices. Each laboratory would normally be zoned into workstations, equipment areas, secure areas and fume cupboards. The logic of service ducting and structural bays determines the precise room layouts. In high-tech research labs full underfloor servicing gives the maximum of flexibility.

Space per researcher is normally dependent upon the level of research undertaken. At a teaching university an allowance is normally made of 1,200 millimetres of worktop length per student, at a typical research university about 2,000 millimetres, at a high performing research university 3–4,000 mm per student. Certain subjects such as biochemistry and microbiology require more worktop space but, because the life of research contracts is normally about three years to five, it is a mistake to invest too heavily in specific layout adaptations. Flexibility and long-life durability of equipment and furniture should be the priority.

Typical laboratory layouts vary between disciplines: linear benching suits subjects such as chemistry while shorter bench arrangements are preferred for computer-based research. In a typical teaching university laboratory there needs to be separate provision for research testing, discussion and demonstration. In a research-based university, long lengths of benching with separate discussion and dissemination rooms nearby work well. Where 'blue skies' research is undertaken space should be set aside for quiet reflection, perhaps as a planted atrium in the building.

As has been discussed, laboratories are among the most hazardous areas on the campus. Hazards come in many

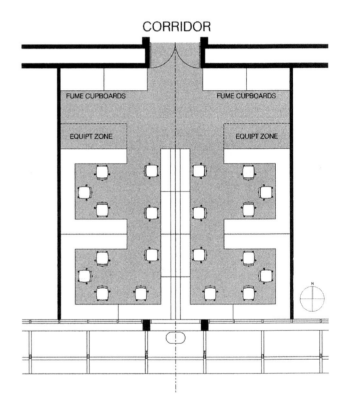

8.11 Workstation layout, Institute of Biomedical Sciences, University of Strathclyde, Glasgow, UK, by Reiach and Hall.

forms – chemical, biohazard, radioactive and electronic. Many health and safety regulations apply as do those concerned with animal welfare. While the priority in laboratory design is that of operational flexibility, safety must not be compromised in the pursuit of efficiency.

In larger universities a separate research quarter on campus is often provided. It may consist of a cluster of different laboratories serving the specific needs of engineering, science or medicine. The research quarter may also serve the research needs of students in the arts, design and humanities. Whatever configuration is employed it is important that students are encouraged to interact across disciplines. In fact much useful research is not in the subjects themselves but in the interface between them. For instance the joining of medical research with design research may lead to a new generation of wheelchairs or support systems for injured backs. Such

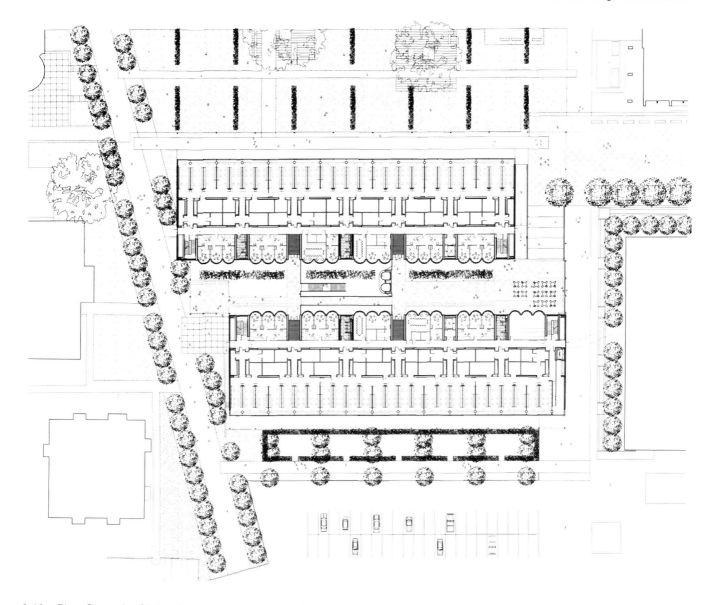

8.12 Plan, Center for Clinical Research Sciences, Stanford University, Palo Alto, USA, by Foster and Partners.

collaboration needs to be fostered by the layout of the campus and the design of laboratory buildings.

Four Case Studies of Research Buildings: a comparison between the USA and UK

(a)   Center for Clinical Research Sciences, Stanford University, Palo Alto, USA

Designed by Foster and Partners, the 11,640 square metre Center for Clinical Research Sciences (1998) at Stanford University combines laboratories, research facilities, offices and the medical school's human anatomy department. The design owes something to the Sir Alexander Fleming Building at Imperial College, London, designed by the same practice and also incorporating a central atrium. Both buildings are lin-

ear in basic form, rationally planned around the rigorous demands of research, yet, in the provision of internal social space, seek to promote the casual exchange of ideas between academics.

The Center for Clinical Research Sciences consists of two parallel laboratories sharing a common atrium in the centre. Externally the building is approached by a generous oversailing louvred canopy three-storeys high which protects the laboratories and offices inside from solar heat gains while providing for effective and even daylight penetration. The Mediterranean quality of climate at Stanford has been exploited to achieve a balance of daylight and solar-assisted ventilation, using a wide full-height atrium to moderate the internal environment. In this space there are cafes, a small library, a planted avenue and high-level bridges which link the two research wings together.

The Dean of Medicine, Dr Eugene Bauer, sought a design which addressed the notion of collaboration because he believed that research discovery comes from the cross-fertilisation of ideas.[2] The two, parallel, four-storey wings consist of three storeys of laboratories sandwiching the atrium with lifts, stairs, ducts and bridges taken along the inside face so that the perimeter can be exploited for lighting and ventilating the laboratories. The upper floor consists of offices arranged flexibly without disrupting the strict demands of the laboratories below.

The environmental strategy is as 'green' as the brief and Palo Alto climate allows. Offices have openable windows and there is a separate air-handling system for the main research areas of the building. The building is aligned north–south so that the demanding east–west elevations are kept to a minimum. This is a strategy which avoids designing the facade to overcome low-angled sunlight, a particular problem for laboratory work. The south elevation is protected from the sun by a massive oversailing cornice of aluminium solar shades with the north elevation smoothly glazed for optimum access to daylight. As a result each facade is distinctively fashioned by the environmental conditions of their different aspects.

The new research facility sits at the junction of various routes across the campus. The masterplan at Stanford is typical of those in the USA, a clear structure of buildings, routes and spaces which leaves little option in architectural layout than to contribute to the order of the whole. Foster's Nigel Dancey, director for the building, welcomes the inherent order commenting that the practice had 'never worked within such an organised masterplan before'.[3] The main route into the new building aligns with the side of an earlier hospital designed in 1959 by Edward Durrell Stone, while forming a planted courtyard to the south.

(b) *Plant Science Center, Purdue University, St Louis, Missouri, USA*

Designed by the UK practice of Nicholas Grimshaw and Partners, the Donald Danforth Plant Science Center (1999) is the product of a number of co-operating universities (Purdue, Illinois, Missouri-Columbia and Washington) and the biochemical company Monsanto. The building consists of two parallel blocks of laboratories separated by an atrium which is crossed by bridges and stairs and overlooked by the projecting galleries of meeting rooms. The £35 million ($60 million) building has a floor area of nearly 17,000 square metres divided into private research laboratories and a semi-public shared atrium. There are also lecture theatres, research library and faculty lounges designed as 'pods' in the central open space.

In basic form there are similarities with Foster and Partner's design for the medical research facilities at Stanford University. Both consist of laboratories divided by a long parallel glazed street which acts as a social and academic focus for mainly research facilities. Both too employ brise-soleil and double facades to moderate the climate, and to provide architectural interest in a building type noted for its anonymity. As with the Stanford building, Grimshaw orientates the St Louis laboratories east–west so that the main

Building	Architect	Special Features	Cost
Center for Clinical Research Sciences, Stanford University	Foster and Partners	• Research laboratory with teaching in basement and offices on top floor • Central atrium for cross fertilisation of research ideas • High level of environmental design in demanding climate • Building which contributes to an ordered masterplan	$4,500/m² (approx) or £2,800/m²

1   Jameson Hall, University of Cape Town, South Africa.

2   Sather Tower by John Galen Howard, University of California, Berkeley, USA.

3   Traditional college architecture in the USA is more concerned with creating utopian communities than its counterpart in Europe (Old Quad, Stanford University, California).

4 (Above) Paul Hamlyn Learning Resource Centre, Thames Valley University, Slough, UK, by Richard Rogers Partnership.

5 (Left) Research centre, University of Marne-La-Vallée, Paris, France, by Jourda and Perraudin.

6 (Above) Computer visualisation, Center for Clinical Research Sciences, Stanford University, Palo Alto, USA, by Foster and Partners.

7 (Right) Facade detail, Science Building, University of Portsmouth, UK, by Jeremy Dixon, Edward Jones.

10 (Right) Concert Hall, Music Academy, Stuttgart, Germany, by Michael Wilford and Partners.

8 (Left) Interior, Lecture Theatre at Kobe Institute, Japan, by Troughton McAslan and Partners.

9 (Below) Music Academy, Stuttgart, Germany, by Michael Wilford and Partners.

11 (Left) Faculty of Design, University of Salford, Manchester, UK, by Hodder Associates.

12 Interior of Street, Faculty of Design, University of Salford, Manchester, UK, by Hodder Associates.

13 Kobe Institute, Japan, by Troughton McAslan.

14 Low-energy student housing, Panns Bank, University of Sunderland, UK, by Feilden Clegg Architects.

15 (Below) Meeting House (1964), University of Sussex, Brighton, UK, by Basil Spence. This was one of the first modern campus buildings to be listed in the UK.

16 (Right) Experiments in ecological design at the University of Sunderland, UK, by Building Design Partnership.

17 (Left) Law library, University of Cambridge, UK, by Foster and Partners.

18 (Below) Paul Hamlyn Learning Resource Centre, Thames Valley University, Slough, UK, by Richard Rogers Partnership.

19 (Left) Student mall, Temasek Polytechnic, Singapore, by Michael Wilford and Partners. The building sends multi-cultural signals in colour, form and detail.

20 (Above) Universities are symbols of hope in depressed areas. University of Lincolnshire and Humberside, Lincoln Campus, UK, by RMJM.

21 (Below) Innovative low-energy Business School, Robert Gordon University, Aberdeen, UK, by Foster and Partners.

22 Jubilee Campus, University of Nottingham, by Michael Hopkins and Partners.

23 Design department, University of Newcastle, New South Wales, Australia, by Stutchbury Pape (2000).

24 New gateway building for Human and Health Sciences at University of Huddersfield, Yorkshire, UK, by Abbey Holford Rowe (1999).

25   Architecture School, University of Newcastle, New South Wales, Australia, by Peter Stutchbury.

26   (Over page) Higher Education signalled by dramatic modern architecture (Temasek Polytechnic, Singapore, by Michael Wilford and Partners).

27   The Jowett Buildings, Balliol College, Oxford.

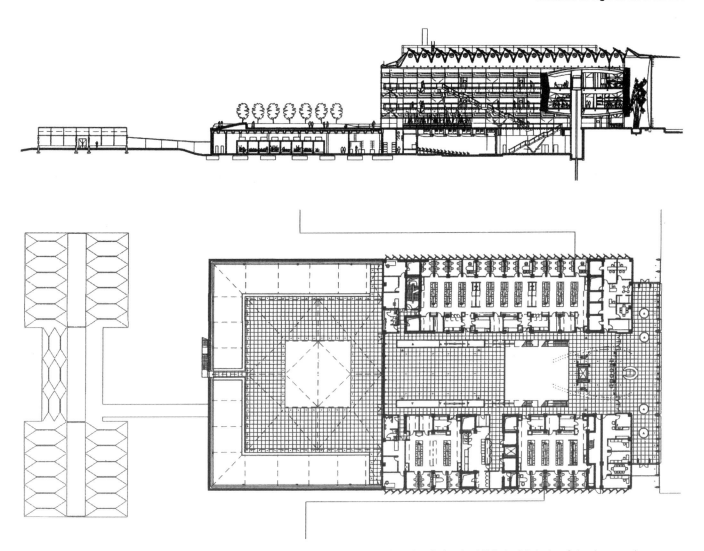

8.13 Plan and section, Donald Danforth Plant Science Center, Purdue University, St Louis, USA, by Nicholas Grimshaw and Partners.

facades face either south or north.

Being a plant science centre, there is a combination of research, education, conference and arts facilities within the same building envelope. The main auditorium and conference rooms are in a semi-basement beneath the labs and atrium. This gives

Building	Architect	Special Features	Cost
Donald Danforth Plant Science Center, Purdue University, St Louis	Nicholas Grimshaw and Partners	• Collaborative research centre between 4 universities • Ecological design • Mixed-mode ventilation aided by solar chimney and powered by photovoltaics	$3,100/m² or £2,060/m²

them easy access to car parks and deliveries. The laboratories above enjoy privacy and security with plant rooms housed on the roof. Perimeter ducts take services around the laboratory and distribute them via raised floors and suspended ceilings.

The atrium is a well planted glazed street with walls of glass at either end and a roof of closely set waves reminiscent of Grimshaw's UK pavilion of 1992 at the Seville Expo. The unusual roof form is generated by the need to maximise passive solar ventilation augmented by secondary heated air from offices and laboratories. A separate glazed corridor running east–west behind the south facade acts as a climate modifier with its motorised louvres powered by photovoltaic cells positioned on the roof.

The Donald Danforth Plant Science Center has been designed to mimic the way plants themselves behave. By layering the facade and encouraging the movement of elements of construction in response to changes in temperature and humidity, the building assumes a bio-

8.14 Section, Sir Alexander Fleming Building, Imperial College, London, UK, by Foster and Partners.

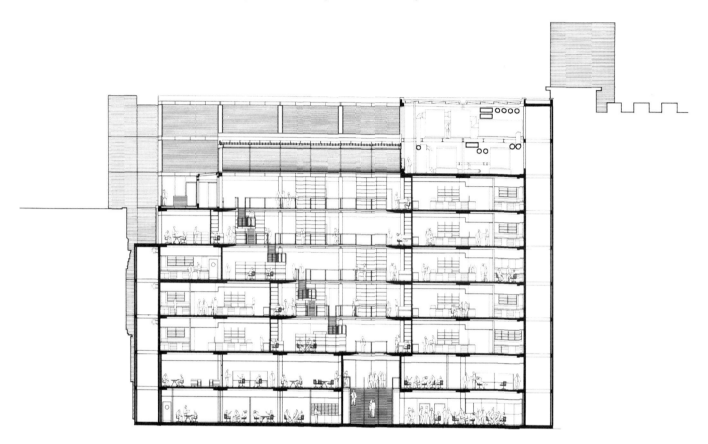

logical character.[4] Ecological principles and space design converge here to produce what is potentially one of the landmark campus buildings of our age.

(c)   Biomedical School, Imperial College, London, UK

The £45 million new Biomedical School (1996), known as Sir Alexander Fleming Building, at Imperial College designed by Foster and Partners provides combined biology and medical facilities at a top ranking research university. The 24,000 square metre accommodation is arranged on seven floors with a central roof-lit atrium. The top three floors are exclusively for postgraduate students and here the main research facilities are located. Services such as air-handling units are located on the roof for flexibility and ease of access.

The laboratories are open plan in order to maximise operational choice by senior management engaged in attracting major commercial research contracts. It is an arrangement which met resistance from research staff who were more familiar with cellular laboratories.[5] Separate writing-up space is provided around the laboratories, positioned in the building to help bridge the research facilities with the teaching accommodation.

Technically this is a sophisticated building. The main lecture theatre is fitted with a fibre-optic link so that lectures can be transmitted live on the internet.[6] This helps project an image of high-tech teaching which the building strives to match, and which Imperial College thinks is vital for the recruitment of topflight students, researchers and senior academics. The image extends to low-energy design as well. A funnel-shaped atrium varies from 20 metres wide at the top to just over 3 metres at the division on level two between undergraduate teaching (below) and research (above). The two zones are sealed for environmental and acoustic reasons with an internal glass ceiling. Effectively the upper floors where the main intellectual work occurs is naturally ventilated via the stack effect and opening sections of the wave-like roof. The lower levels where teaching and lecture theatres are located are ventilated by more conventional means. A concrete frame is employed, rather than steel, in order to moderate temperature rises and to provide the stability against vibration for the sensitive electron microscopes.[7]

8.15 Sir Alexander Fleming Building, Imperial College, London, UK, by Foster and Partners.

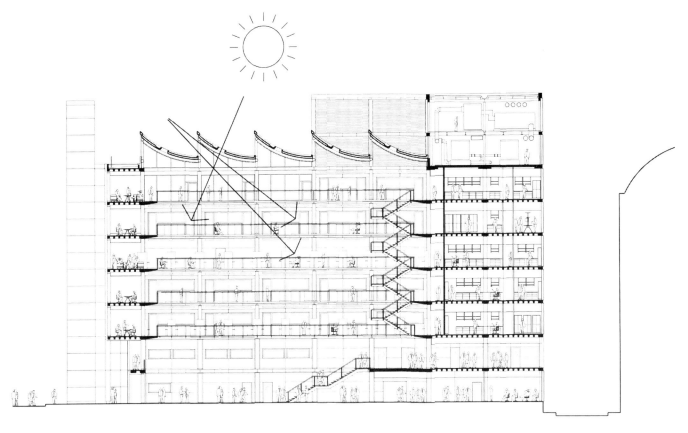

Building	Architect	Special Features	Cost
Biomedical School, Imperial College, London (known as Sir Alexander Fleming Building)	Foster and Partners	• Low-energy strategy based upon central atrium • Open-plan laboratories to encourage intellectual interaction and flexibility • Zoning of building vertically into teaching and research • Social space in the centre, research space at periphery	£1,870/m²

The Biomedical School combines research and teaching within the same building. The atrium with its finely diffused natural light and louvres of aluminium creates a dramatic focus for the activities of the building. Offices, seminar rooms and student writing-up space are located on terraces overlooking the atrium, with the laboratory space positioned at the periphery of the building. As in many research facilities the atrium provides both environmental and social space – the interaction of air flow as well as ideas.

(d)   Science Building, University of Portsmouth, UK

This Science Building (1995), desgned by Jeremy Dixon and Edward Jones, is an extension to an existing building and is necessarily compromised by context. It is not a rational container for research but a landmark at a crucial street corner on the campus of the University of Portsmouth. The building fills the site by compacting the various elements (laboratories, lecture theatre, staff offices) into a slick aluminium-clad enclosure. The agglomeration of parts normally kept separate in such buildings gives a sculptural quality from the outside and rich and complex spaces on the inside.

The building does not follow the precedent set by Louis Kahn's Richards Medical Research Building, University of Pennsylvannia, Philadelphia (1957–60),

8.16 (Right) Facade detail, Science Building, University of Portsmouth, UK, by Jeremy Dixon, Edward Jones.

Building	Architect	Special Features	Cost
Science Building, University of Portsmouth	Jeremy Dixon Edward Jones	• Urban landmark • Highly serviced throughout • Celebration of public areas • Differentiation between teaching and research laboratories	Not available

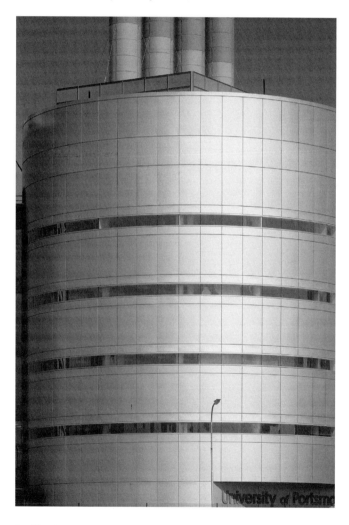

8.16 (Right) Facade detail, Science Building, University of Portsmouth, UK, by Jeremy Dixon, Edward Jones.

of well-articulated 'served' and 'servant' spaces', an approach adopted in most of the earlier examples in this chapter. Instead, the whole building is highly serviced with a section which recalls that of a power station or ocean liner. Each part except the lecture theatre has access to service ducts through floor and ceiling, providing a high level of flexibility for future change. The laboratories are split between those used for teaching which sit above the curved lecture theatre, and those employed primarily for research. The latter are rectangular and unspecific in layout, reflecting the unpredictable nature of science research.[8]

The public spaces of the building are seen as an important part of the pedagogic experience. The foyer, stairs and gathering spaces alongside the main lecture theatre are generous in spirit and scale. This is a building which looks superficially like an aluminium drinks can, yet it is a sophisticated response to the challenge of urban context and internal research programme.

Notes

1. Robert Steel, 'The Strathclyde Institute' *Prospect,* Autumn 1998, p 51. See also James Burland 'Controlled experiment', *RIBA Journal,* January 1999, pp 30–7.

2. *The Architects' Journal,* 3 September 1998, p 24.
3. Ibid.
4. David Taylor, 'Grimshaw Grows in America', *The Architects' Journal,* 26 August 1999, p 6.
5. Andy Cook, 'Enlightenment', *Building,* 24 October 1997, p 61.
6. Ibid.
7. Ibid, p 63.
8. Sheila O'Donnell, 'Building: Surface Tension', *Architecture Today,* AT 70.29, July 1996.

Special functions: special forms

The typical campus contains special buildings which have evolved to serve students from across the university. The sports hall, lecture theatre block and catering facilities are normally distinctive structures which help landmark the campus. Sometimes, because of their special needs, medical schools serve the same function. Like the library, these buildings have their own locational dictates and need to be planned as part of pedestrian movement systems across the university estate. Being major magnets of student life, such buildings are often treated architecturally as landmarks. They always deserve special attention.

Sports halls and physical recreation

Sport has long been associated with academic life. The development of the mind has often been accompanied by a parallel interest in physical recreation. There are many reasons for this – the classical ideal of unity between intellectual and physical pursuits, the social benefits of team sports to student development,

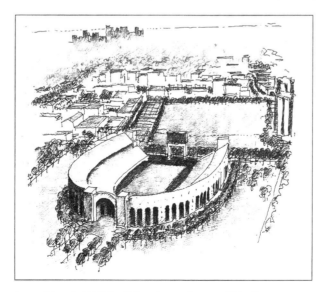

9.1 Sketch (1927) of historic stadium at Ohio State University, Columbus, USA. from 1995 masterplan by Sasaki Associates and Michael Dennis Associates.

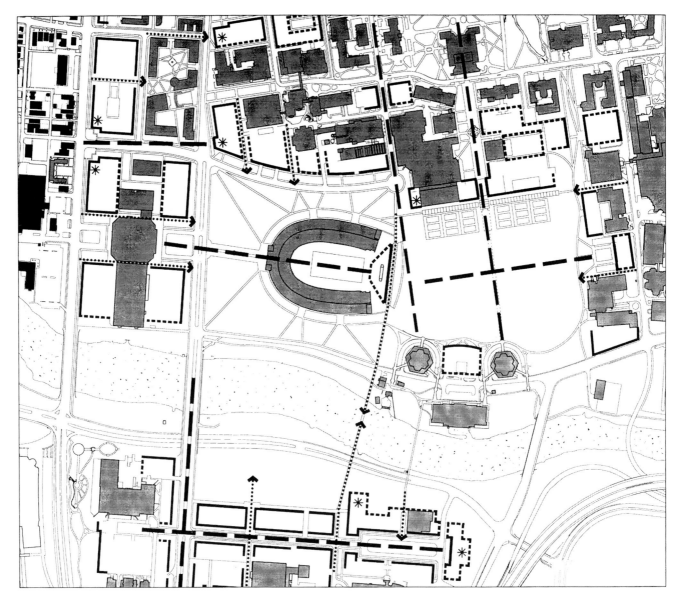

9.2 Distinctive shape of stadium enhanced by new framing buildings in 1995 campus masterplan by Sasaki Associates and Michael Dennis Associates. Ohio State University, Columbus, USA.

the prestige associated with a successful university sports team (particularly strong in the USA), and the use of sport as a way of relieving stress for staff and students alike.

The range of sporting facilities varies from large enclosed sports halls to open stadia, playing fields and running tracks. Since these are all space demanding and have specific dimensions which can rarely be altered, they form important elements of any campus masterplan. Also, being large and conspicuous buildings, sports facilities need careful consideration in terms of urban design.

As a general rule sports facilities occupy the periphery of the campus. Here they can be reached readily by car, tram or bus; there is space for future expansion; sports buildings and playing fields can be closely integrated; and being at the edge, sports buildings can be designed as landmarks without competing with the academic centre. The techni-

cal demands of sports hall and stadia can generate exciting buildings. The wide-span roofs of gymnasia and multi-purpose halls, and the daring cantilevers of the typical sports stadia, lead to great architectural possibilities. Also, being often round in shape, or in the case of the sports hall a simple rectangle, the formal simplicity of the buildings can generate elegant solutions.

The university campus plan should therefore seek to exploit the compositional opportunities offered by physical recreation. The buildings and playing fields impose a geometric and structural order upon the landscape. This can be pleasing if landscape design and building design are well integrated. Planting is important not just as a unifying element but as a means of screening the inevitable expanses of car parking which accompany sports buildings.

9.3 Sports Hall, University of Cape Town, South Africa.

Sports halls are large-span, voluminous buildings generally without windows. They can be lumpen and uninviting or, if the structural frame and panels of construction are expressed, welcoming and well proportioned. The entrance doors offer relief from the sense of physical enclosure and should be signalled by careful design. Canopies, ramps and double-height doors all help identify the entrance and celebrate arrival.

At a detailed level, sports halls are usually column free in order to offer choice in internal layout. Structural columns not only impede flexibility of use but pose a danger to users. Windows where they exist are normally at high level, sometimes positioned in the roof. Since sport at a university is both concerned with physical prowess and social interaction, there is usually a cafe or bar plus extensive spectating facilities.

Fully enclosed stadia are rarely a feature of campuses outside the USA but many universities have stands for watching sport. With seating for up to five thousand, these small stadia offer the opportunity to create distinctive buildings, sometimes at the gateway to the campus. The use of suspended or cantilevered construction in steel, timber or concrete provides the means of architectural display above the head of spectators. Where intercollegiate sports are strong, building design has an important role to play in enhancing the competitive spirit between universities.

Where the sports facilities are extensive they form a natural recreational 'village'. Here the task is one of establishing a coherent urban grouping out of somewhat disparate buildings (sports hall, gymnasia, stadia, swimming pool, changing rooms). The Lynchian principles of 'district identity' provide useful guiding rules, eg establishing centre, edge, node and character driven by functional demands.[1]

The imperative of flexibility

University sports halls differ from civic ones in the higher degree of flexibility required of academic recreation provision. This is partly the result of the openness universities are expected to show towards new forms of leisure, sport and recreation, and partly the way in which sport and academic study are frequently linked. This is particularly true of universities in the USA where sports degrees are relatively common and, even for other students, physical recreation plays a large part in university life.

Over the past fifty years sport has moved indoors. Even where outdoor pitches occur a great deal of training takes place indoors, and many traditional sports, such as soccer and hockey, have adapted their rules to indoor conditions. This adds to the pressure to create flexible provision as does the need to use the sports hall for fitness training via aerobics and step dancing. A typical university sports hall consists of a wide variety of spaces, wet and dry, enclosed and open. Different sports can be accommodated to a degree by different line markings but many sports, such as squash, require physical enclosure. Hence walls cannot be eliminated even when planning flexibility is paramount. Columns must, of course, be avoided for safety reasons but can occur between participant and spectator areas, between the sports hall and swimming pool or between hall and changing rooms. The elimination of columns leads to wide-span structures which, usually constructed in steel or concrete, create distinctive landmarks and dramatic interior spaces. Added to the demands

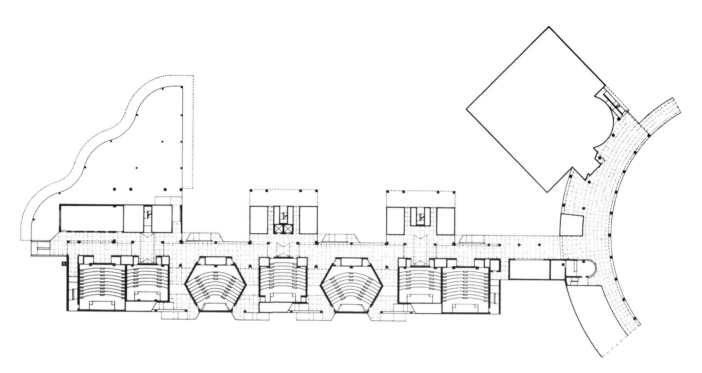

of wide-span structures is the need for even, preferably natural light, which can add further to opportunities for architectural expression.

Spectator provision and facilities for participants should be segregated. This leads to separate entrances and concourses serving the needs of each. Viewing galleries are often built above changing rooms, squash courts or practice rooms; sometimes a central gallery leads to dry sports on one side and wet sports on the other. Where a central concourse exists it can provide useful structural support for the roof and, with a stepped section, it allows the penetration of natural light into the centre of the building.

Lecture theatres

Most universities contain a centralised block of lecture theatres often with direct links to large examination halls or student catering facilities. The amount of lecture theatre provision depends upon the nature and traditions of a university – for example, in France formal lecturing is more common than in the UK – and there is a different balance between central and faculty provision. Where lecture theatres are provided in concentrated form they normally consist of a block of up to six theatres of varying size seating between fifty and 250 students. In all cases modern AV and IT networks are essential. Fire escape, noise and sight lines have similar technical requirements to public theatre and cinema provision.

Architecturally, centralised lecture theatre provision provides the opportunity for creating visually dramatic

9.4 Various shapes of lecture theatre employed in School of Business, Temasek Polytechnic, Singapore, by Michael Wilford and Partners.

9.5 Variety of lecture theatres employed at Helsinki Technical University, Finland, by Alvar Aalto (1953).

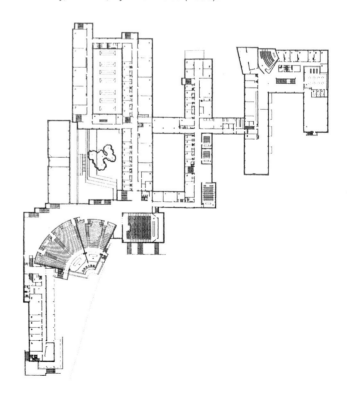

9.6 (Left) Distinctive lecture theatre entrance, Temasek Polytechnic, Singapore, by Michael Wilford and Partners.

9.7 (Below) Educatorium, Utrecht, Holland, by Rem Koolhaas/OMA.

buildings using the solidity of such buildings to create sculpture on the campus. Where lecture theatres sit below a floor of restaurants, as in the French case study at the University of Marne-la-Valée, the contrast between mass and transparency can be eyecatching.

Two Case Studies of Lecture Theatre Design

(a) Educatorium, University of Utrecht, The Netherlands

A typical example of integrated provision is the Educatorium (1995), designed by Rem Koolhaas of OMA, a building in the Uithof district on the edge of

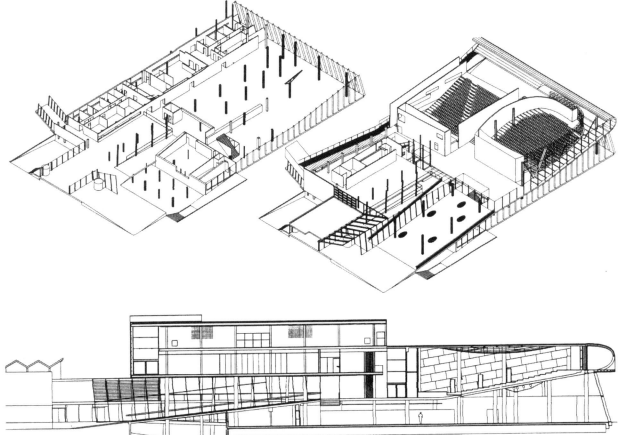

Utrecht, which houses the central functions of the university – lecture theatres, examination halls and restaurant – in a single building. It is a major addition to the masterplan prepared in 1986 by Koolhaas and tests the architect's thesis, which he borrowed from Leon Battista Alberti, that a big building should be designed as a small city.

The Educatorium is complex in form and equally complex in theory. Koolhaas' philosophy of 'bigness' expressed as a continuous, folded undifferentiated urban agglomeration of functions finds reality in this university building. There is no attempt to give separate form to the main parts, instead all the functions share a common envelope of angled walls, ramps, interconnecting floors and ceilings. This is not to say that the building lacks legibility, for with practice it is easy to orientate oneself, rather the aim is to create the tension and drama of the city in a single building.

A grand entrance vestibule is the focus of the Educatorium. Links from other nearby buildings converge here as ramps or high-level bridges forming a cruciform of internal accommodation. The circulation areas interconnect just as streets in cities do, provid-ing a choice of route and the opportunity for chance encounter. Routes are not corridors but cuts through the slab of the building. As a result the circulation areas have sides without parallel geometry, ceilings of variable height and floors of variable angles. By way of contrast the main accommodation – lecture theatres and examination halls – is placed within rational shells. These are allowed to impinge upon the interiors, giving a clue to function, and to impact upon the exterior, giving the building interest to the street. The collisions of form, geometry and structural order have their own logic and can be justified on a compositional level. They may perhaps be hard to square with the usual, at least in the UK, logic of buildability and operational flexibility found. The design, however, creates a notable landmark in an unpromising university quarter on the outskirts of Utrecht. To make a monument out of necessity is a virtue which many universities have displayed in the past. Here Koolhaas challenges recent wisdom, returning university architecture to the arena of philosophical speculation. This, afterall, was the starting point for Wren, Jefferson, Kahn and Stirling.

(b) *Lecture theatre and restaurant building, University of Marne-la-Vallée, Paris, France*

This is another example of lecture theatre provision being turned into a campus landmark. The dramatic new building acts as a powerful gateway to the new University at Marne-la-Vallée outside Paris (1992). It contains five lecture theatres on the ground floor with a restaurant and food hall above. The geometry of the buildings, designed by Françoise Jourda and Gilles Perraudin, draws upon the configuration of the site, especially the path of student movement across the campus. The ship-like form deflects movement with the prow of the lecture theatre directing students to staircases and concourses without the need to negotiate right-angled turns.

This building is a study in slipstream movement systems and draws upon nautical metaphors and forms to handle the flood of students who arrive or

Building	Architect	Special Features	Cost
Educatorium, University of Utrecht	Rem Koolhaas/ OMA	• Building which itself engages in intellectual inquiry • Large complex meeting spaces • Large building designed as a small city • Landmark to uplift featureless educational neighbourhood	Not available

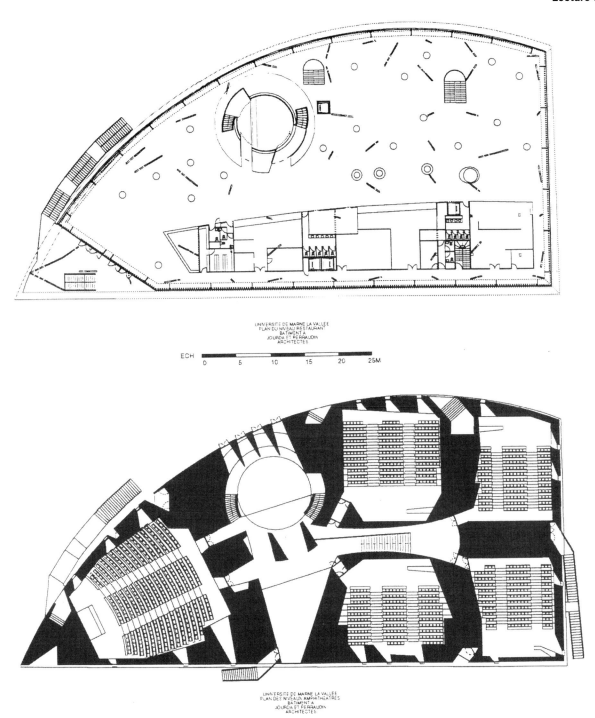

9.8 Plan, lecture theatre (below) and restaurant (above), University of Marne-La-Vallée, Paris, France, by Jourda and Perraudin.

leave at much the same time. The five lecture the-atres are grouped about a large, central, circular foyer which both gathers the eight hundred students who can be present at any single time and directs them to their lectures. The movement space is carved out of the block with the volumes reflecting the geometry of space syntax. At the entrance to the lecture theatres there are large areas in which to wait, a clever reflec-tion not just of preparing for the lecture but of the social discourse which necessarily accompanies stu-dent life. It is a subtlety often overlooked in the pro-vision of concentrated lecture theatres.

The building captures the priority attached in French university education to the formal lecture. The lec-tures take place in highly controlled environments with little contact with the outside world. The emphasis

Building	Architect	Special Features	Cost
Lecture theatre, and restaurant, University of Marne-la-Vallée, Paris	Jourda and Perraudin	• Dramatic gateway • Groups five lecture theatres with restaurant above • Architectural discourse of a philosophical nature • Building which promotes social and academic exchange	£5 million in 1992

upon the word of the professor is paramount, yet the lecture theatres are not without visual interest. In each case a slight alteration in the layout or alignment of walls gives a tension to the space – a condition which can enhance the learning experience.

The restaurant and food hall floor above is the converse of that below. Whereas the restaurant is open, transparent and dynamic, the lecture theatre floor is enclosed, reflective and cerebral. After their lectures the students rise through a choice of staircase, both internal and external, to the restaurant level. Columns are angled and apparently randomly located, creating an impression of carefreeness. Food is dispensed from a long counter which is again somewhat ship-like in shape and sail-like in detail. The walls are almost continuously glazed allowing views out and, after dark, give the restaurant the effect of a beacon on campus.

This building is the major landmark on the modernist campus at Marne-la-Vallée, a new town outside Paris. Its form and plan are quite unlike that of other buildings at the university, providing visual punctuation which reinforces the distinctive function. As a landmark it both orientates visitors, defines routes and   signals, through a spectacular combination of forms, its special programme.

Medical schools

Where medical faculties are large and partly autonomous they should be positioned in the campus masterplan as independent urban complexes. This is the preferred pattern for major medical schools which tend to perform two roles – training for health care professionals and providing a medical service for the local community. This duality of function gives the medical school a quite different relationship to the university than other faculties. There are two common groupings for the medical school: either as a self-contained entity within the overall campus (as at Stanford, Nottingham and Sheffield), or as a physically related but still separate health care village at the edge of the main campus (as at Cape Town, Dublin and Edinburgh).

Medical schools have demanding patterns of vehicle use (emergency, staff, visitors) which mean that they generally have their own road system. The incompatability of combining the vehicles of both the university and medical school is one reason why separate access and location tends to occur. Another is the fashion in which medical schools grow. The hospital is a much stressed building type: new medical technologies and changing health-care

9.9   Medical School, Stanford University, Palo Alto, USA, by Hoover Associates.

9.10 European Institute of Health and Medical Science, University of Surrey, Guilford, UK, by Nicholas Grimshaw and Partners.

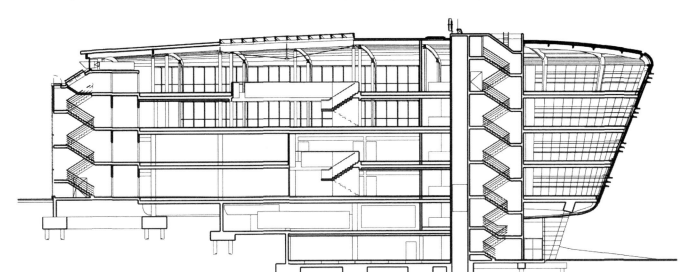

management puts the teaching hospital under perpetual pressure for internal change and external growth. Sir Herbert Baker who prepared the plan for the medical school at Cape Town University in 1920 said that such facilities tended to 'grow like prickly pairs'. The implication for Baker was twofold: first to prepare a strong masterplan to accommodate inevitable growth, and second to choose a site where growth of the medical faculty would not disrupt the orderly development of the university.

Too much space between the university and medical school means that the sharing of libraries, sports facilities and halls of residence is not possible. Hence, the ideal situation is one where the journey on foot between the centre of the campus and the medical school is under ten minutes. This is the arrangement at Glasgow University where the journey to the various medical buildings is along well-lit pedestrian promenades. Since the education of nurses occurs in many medical schools, questions of safety and security for students moving between buildings after dark is paramount.

Hospitals and their associated medical schools require well-managed systems for dealing with toxic and virological wastes. Radiological contamination, the health threats from discarded syringes and swabs, and other sources of pollution all need careful thought at the planning stage. The system of pedestrian movement and that of servicing the buildings needs physical segregation and should not violate safety at the university campus. As a consequence, the university masterplan and that of the medical school and teaching hospital needs to be evolved in parallel.

Case Study

Human and Health Sciences Building, University of Huddersfield, UK

The new Human and Health Sciences Building, designed by Abbey Holford Rowe, at the University of Huddersfield (1998) acts as a gateway building to the campus as well as pro-

9.11 Human and Health Sciences Building, University of Huddersfield, UK, by Abbey Holford Rowe.

viding general and specialised teaching space. It is arranged as an L-shaped building of two unequal sized wings with an oval reception lodge positioned in the angle. The reception lodge leads to an atrium 5 metres wide which runs through the four-storey height of the building and acts as an informal social and teaching space overlooked by each floor.

Adaptability and ease of maintenance underpins the design philosophy. A steel frame based upon alternate 6 metre and 7.5 metre bays was adopted for flexibility, speed of construction and suitability for meeting the dual demands of teaching and research. The building is 18 metres deep with a central corridor and perimeter accommodation. To give flexibility for service runs there is a floated concrete slab supported by steel 'hollorib' decking with access to the service void reached via the suspended ceiling. At ground level there is a raised access floor of 100 millimetres between the finished floor level and service slab. To provide flexibility in room layout a combination of metal stud and blockwork partitioning has been employed, based upon a sub grid of 1.5 metres.

The two main constraints upon flexibility were the availability of natural light and ventilation. A plan depth of 18 metres provides an optimum balance for both within the cost limits of fan assisted ventilation. The atrium plays a key part in terms of energy use and ventilation, and is angled to maximise daylight penetration without unwanted solar gain. A restaurant with a curved balcony overlooks the atrium, providing animation near the point of entry to the building.

The building is repetitive in basic structural form irrespective of detailed planning requirements. Since teaching, learning and research in the health services evolve more rapidly than most academic disciplines, the building layout is kept simple. Two service towers containing vertical service ducts, lifts and toilets rise through the building and connect in terms of air handling with the corridors and suspended ceilings. Two complementary glazed stair towers mark the extremities of each wing, providing fire escapes between floors as well as visual termination to the building.

The building provides 4,800 square metres of accommodation while also acting as the first point of contact for visitors to the university. This dual role helps justify the oval pavilion within its embrace, and the forming of a square between it and older neighbours. Seen from the busy ring road which separates the Huddersfield University campus from the town centre, the building provides an effective gateway to the university. As an exemplar of best practice in the provision of special teaching accommodation it offers two lessons: first, that some buildings need to perform campus-wide duties as well as satisfying programmatic requirements, second, that flexibility and architectural statement are not incompatible.

Note

1. Lynchian principles from Kevin Lynch, *The Image of the City*, (1960), MIT, Cambridge, Mass.

Building	Architect	Special Features	Cost
Human and Health Sciences Building, University of Huddersfield	Abbey Holford Rowe	• New gateway to campus	£1,086/m²
		• 18 m plan depth adopted for environmental and construction efficiency	
		• Steel frame partitions for flexibility	
		• Sandstone finish to maintain regional tradition	
		• Atrium as social space with over-looking restaurant	

Art, design and music departments

CHAPTER

10

The education of students in the creative disciplines is playing an increasing part in the life of universities. Art, design and music courses account for around 15-20 per cent of modern university provision. This expansion is partly the result of the broadening portfolio of design courses currently available (industrial, product, computer-aided, fashion) and also the trend towards courses which are of a vocational nature. While music and architecture are traditional subjects taught, these often form the disciplinary core for the development of new courses in performance art, theatre design, multi-media and creative imaging.

What distinguishes art, design and music education is the importance attached to the studio. There is a corresponding concentration upon project work and with it the development of the traditional skills of drawing, in the case of design, and instrumentation in the case of music. The studio is where much learning takes place, but it is also a social arena and a performance space. This is particularly true in art, design and architectural

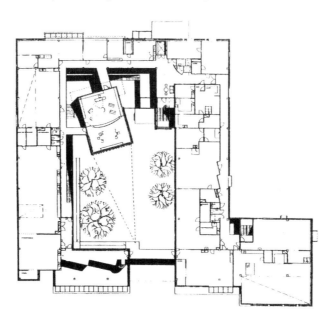

10.1   Art School, Kankaanpaa, Finland, by Kouvo and Partanen.

10.2 Power Centre for the Performing Arts, University of Michigan, Ann Arbor, USA, by Roche and Dinkeloo.

education where the studio is the 'crit' space in which students present and defend their projects in the company of student peers and tutors. Unlike general teaching accommodation in universities, the studio is a place to develop, display and defend ideas generated by students working in a range of materials such as paint, board, metals and CAD.

In the case of music and theatre, the practice, rehearsal and performance space is vital also to their education. Since much performance is of a team nature, such space helps promote interaction, co-operation and collective creativity. As with the art and design studio, the performance room has special technical characteristics involving acoustics, sight lines and instrument storage. In both design and music, therefore, the space provided has to be of a special nature: no ordinary teaching accommodation will suffice. The studio is normally tall with north lighting and plenty of uninterrupted wall space for hanging work. Peripheral areas are needed in the form of workshops, CAD laboratories, washing and mixing rooms, and small group teaching spaces. The tradition of the personal work bay means that large studios need to be capable of temporary subdivision to suit the requirements of individual or group working. The fine art studio tends to enjoy greater space, especially height, than the design studio, but the latter is generally better served with technical aids of various kinds such as CAD, light tables and tripod-mounted cameras.

Since around 50 per cent of assessment for art and design degrees is based upon project work, the studio needs to sup-

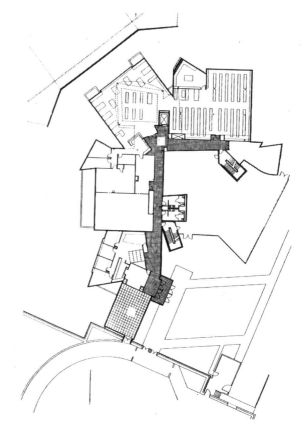

10.3 Art School, Toledo University, USA, by Frank Gehry Associates.

120

10.4 Axonometic, Lyon Architecture School, Vaulx-en-Velin, France, by Jourda and Perraudin.

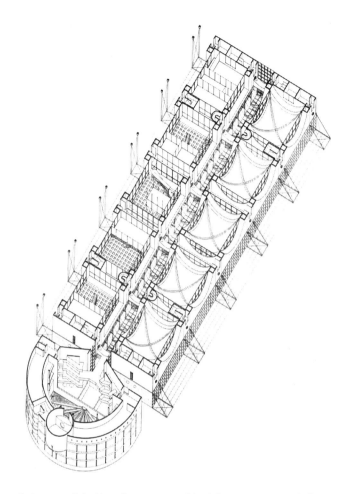

port the making of objects or designs as well as their display. Project work is often called 'deep learning' since it involves an element of integration, penetration and originality. In the design field, the project is frequently undertaken by a group of students, sometimes drawn from different design or craft backgrounds. Team working and extensive periods of occupation of studios are both requirements of accommodation for design education. The emphasis upon project work means that the studio becomes the centre of the academic community. Just as the lecture theatre supports learning in the social sciences, the laboratory the physical sciences, it is the studio which is crucial to course culture in art and design. And the studio has special requirements of height, quality of light, access to services and ambience which standard space auditing often fails to recognise. An adequate brief for the generation of new art and design facilities needs to recognise these conditions.

The music studio too has its own characteristics which have to be met if education in the subject is to flourish. Performance is the culmination of music education yet it requires hours of painstaking practice. The practice rooms require standards of space and sound transmission far in excess of the yardsticks provided in teaching space elsewhere. Where courses have a high element of composition and interactive working with related disciplines such as theatre arts, the accommodation needs to be tailored to interdisciplinary needs.

In both design, theatre and music education, special value is attached to the craft of the discipline – drawing and painting in the case of art and design; instrument skills in the case of music; oration and acting in the case of theatre. Although the trend in higher education is away from craft in favour of academic discourse, the skill development element of these courses remains high. The studio is vital to the culture of these disciplines whether given the name of a performance space, theatre or gallery. Such space supports skill development as well as skill delivering; it is where work is displayed or performed for the wider community. Hence it generally provides a learning environment while also providing the means of public presentation. This adds further to the technical demands made upon the space and

distances it further from general training accommodation. Just as with science laboratories and medical schools, the specificness of design and music accommodation inhibits flexibility of provision and adds to cost.

Since the characteristics of space are specific to the type of courses delivered, there is often a correspondence between the plan of accommodation and the structure of courses. For example, the architecture school, at Vaulx-en-Velin, near Lyon, designed by Jourda and Perraudin (1988) reflects clearly in the plan the five years of education required and the important social and pedagogic role of the 'crit' studio. The central studio running through the architecture school mirrors the lawn in Thomas Jefferson's plan for the University of Virginia – both are symbolic rather than functional. The same is true of the design by Walter Gropius for the Bauhaus (1926–30) at Dessau which replicated in both plan and detail the principles of design education promulgated at the time. The studios and workshops were joined by bridges which acted as intellectual links between abstract design and craft manufacture.

The buildings for teaching the ever broadening portfolio of courses which have been described as the new 'culture industries' require a combination of subject specific accommodation and more general teaching and office space. However, to ignore the particular demands of sub-

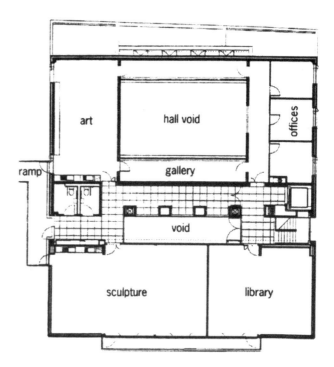

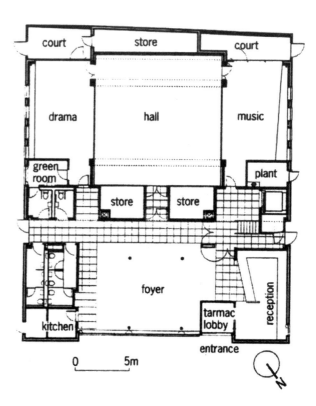

jects such as fine art, theatre and music in the provision of special types of accommodation is to impoverish courses. Studios and performance space are expensive to build and maintain, and lack flexibility of alternative use. But without such accommodation the particular needs of the art, design and music subjects will not be met, undermining academic potential and distancing the university environment from the areas where these subjects are practised in the outside world. On the other hand, the tailored provision of accommodation for these subjects, although expensive, can produce buildings of distinction on campus. In this sense the art and design faculty building becomes a true billboard for the subject.

Two Case Studies

(a) *The Richard Attenborough Centre for Disability and the Arts, University of Leicester, UK*

Designed by architects Bennetts Associates, the Richard Attenborough Centre (1996) is for art students with disabilities. It provides education in the visual arts, dance, drama and music, thanks to a personal contribution from the actor Richard Attenborough

10.6 Plan (first floor above, ground floor below) Richard Attenborough Centre, University of Leicester, UK, by Bennetts Associates.

and a grant from the UK Lottery Board. The commission was won in competition by Bennetts which presented a fifteen-minute tape-recorded walk through the imaginary building as part of the submission.[1] The building is simple and nearly symmetrical in plan in order to aid movement by blind users. Legibility and tactile use of materials underpins the design philosophy. The aim is to forge different environmental conditions (visual and acoustic) in each room in oder to aid orientation by those with visual or hearing difficulties.[2]

The choice of materials seeks to provide good tonal and textural contrast. Colour where employed is bright and restricted to areas such as corridors where navigation is needed. Good lighting is essential and dictates the form of the section as much as the plan. The painting and sculpture galleries located on the upper floor bring in natural light mainly via the roof or at high level through clerestoreys. The music and dance studios on the lower floor expand into a large doubleheight rehearsal hall which acts as the social focus for the Centre.

Since students with disabilities use the facilities at the Centre as well as those elsewhere on campus, the design caters well for movement at the perimeter of the building. There are no steps or changes of level at entrances, doors are wide for wheelchair access, finishes are non-slip and light is orchestrated to define the threshold sequence of functional zones.

The Richard Attenborough Centre is the first purpose-built arts facility in the UK for university students with disabilities. It is attuned to the senses, simple to comprehend and easy to operate. Navigation via the perception and psychology of space is at the core of the design philosophy. Light, colour, texture and space are synchronised, with sunlight adding sparkle in some of the key volumes. Although a building for students with impairment, it is accessible to all. Exhibitions and performance make this an asset for the whole campus and a worthy signal to the wider academic community of the importance of the disabled student.

Building	Architect	Special Features	Cost
Richard Attenborough Centre, University of Leicester	Bennetts Associates	• Purpose built arts facility for disabled students • Light, colour and texture used to provide legibiity • Exhibition as well as teaching space • Lottery funded in part	£1,033/m²

(b)   Faculty of Design, University of Salford, Manchester, UK

The Faculty of Design (1995) at Manchester's Salford University started its life as the school of electronics, engineering and industrial design. However, during the design of the building, a change in management priorities led to it being adapted to the university's new centre for design education. The typology of the building is simple: a central street separates two types of accommodation – pairs of seminar rooms to one side and lecture theatres, workshops, large studios and offices to the other. The architects, Hodder Associates, cleverly distinguish between the rational and the irregular, placing the former to the south side of the long glazed central street and the latter to the north side where environmental conditions are ideal. It is a plan which allows the southern elevation to be protected from sun penetration by the use of simple external blinds, and the north facing large studios and workshops to enjoy neutral northern light.

The central street acts as environmental modifier and social space as well as the means of accessing the various accommodation. The street is narrow and high, giving this space a tension which seems to support the idea of design education. It is in effect

Art, design and music departments

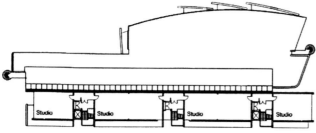

THIRD FLOOR PLAN

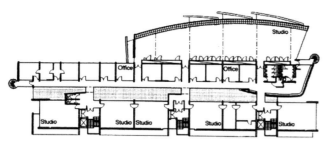

SECOND FLOOR PLAN

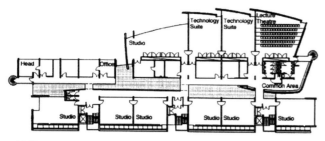

FIRST FLOOR PLAN

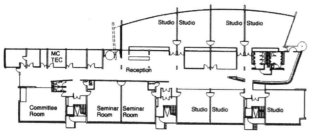

GROUND FLOOR PLAN

10.7 Plan, Faculty of Design, University of Salford, Manchester, UK, by Hodder Associates.

Building	Architect	Special Features	Cost
Faculty of Design, University of Salford, Manchester	Hodder Associates	• Design faculty which expresses in the building the design disciplines	£861/m^2 in 1995
		• Concern for 'street life' in the building	
		• Functional, social and environmental conditions intergrated	
		• Forms new square with older neighbours	

a 'catwalk', crossed by bridges which provide linear views of students and, through the glass partition walls, into the studios themselves. Unlike central streets in research buildings with their air of tranquility and often generous planting, this space talks the language of creativity.

The studios are by way of contrast more rational. They are either, in the case of the smaller studios, paired with clear distinction between 'served' and 'servant' spaces, or, in the large studio, expansive volumes with projecting bow-shaped perimeter walls. The departure from rectilinear orthodoxy helps animate the facades, especially that facing the newly

formed square between old and new neighbours. It also provides orientation for visitors, many of whom use the building as a result of taking electives in design while pursuing studies in other disciplines.

The complex plan and section reflects the dialogue in the brief between rational order and the creation of a special place for design education. Hodder's design also acknowledges the importance of 'street life' to the creative disciplines, but being Manchester with its unpredictable climate, the street is an interior world protected and overlooked by studio activity. The building offers one further lesson. The technology of construction is not hidden but exposed, with the detail expressing the nature of the materials employed. In this sense the ethos of the building is expressed not just in the whole but in the smallest assembly. It is a building not only to use but to learn from.

Notes

1. *The Architects' Journal,* 29 May 1997, p 24.
2. Ibid, p 25.

General teaching space

C H A P T E R

11

Most universities consist of three main types of accommodation:

(a) Specific buildings, such as libraries, with unique functional needs.
(b) Non-specific buildings, such as general teaching space or laboratories, which share generic criteria.
(c) Student or staff housing.

Although each needs to accommodate some change over time, the generic teaching, office and administrative buildings provide great opportunity to design for flexibility at the outset. Since normally between 50–60 per cent of a modern university is general teaching space, this is the area where the concept of functional change through the provision of rational structural and service systems is normally to be found.

Flexibility through building design

The main means by which flexibility is achieved is by adopting narrow but long building plans. This allows for the maximum of natural light and cross ventilation, provides good views out for staff and students, and permits the development of column-free interiors. Using a standard building width of 13–15 metres and a structural module of 7–8 metres, the configuration of general teaching space becomes a series of constructional compartments of about 15 x 7.5 metres. This allows for a further planning grid for partitions, service runs, furniture or lab desks, of 1.5 metres. Periodically, the main teaching space is then divided by vertical towers which provide lifts, stairs, service stacks and lateral stability. It is a recipe developed and exploited in various campus developments by the UK practice of RMJM.

Normally such buildings are constructed of a concrete frame of columns and beams with ceilings left unclad for maximising thermal capacity. Building services are also frequently exposed in order to facilitate changes in pipe runs and wiring without disturbing finishes. Ease of access to building services leads to the adoption of self-contained service systems which can be constructed

General teaching space

11.1   Elevation of Lincoln campus centre, University of Lincolnshire and Humberside, UK, by RMJM.

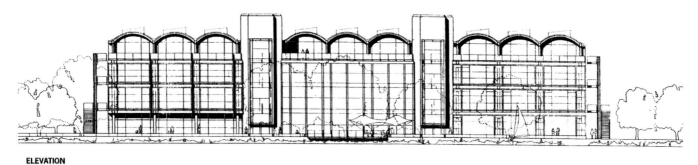

ELEVATION

11.2   Plan, Kobe Institute, Japan, by Troughton McAslan.

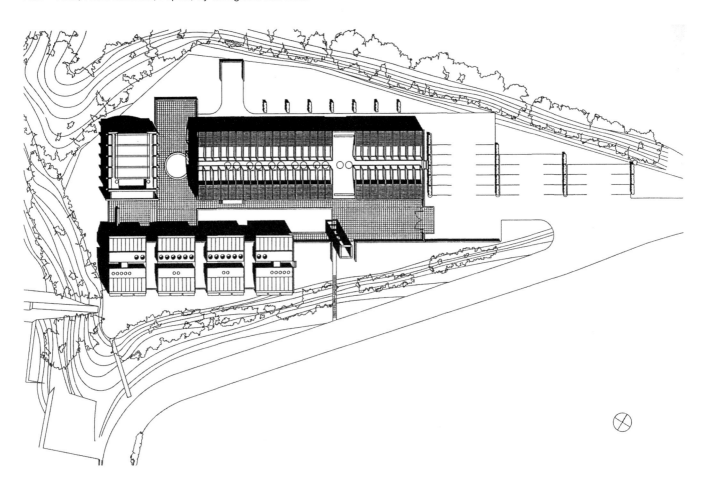

independently of the main contracting process. Since functional change puts greater stress on electrical and environmental services than space, the separation of both at building and infrastructure level makes design sense. Non-specific buildings need to be able to change from open space to cellular space configurations, and from teaching to general office and certain types of laboratory use, such as language and computing. They need, therefore, a high level of electronic cabling accessed via the floor or perimeter ducting. General teaching space needs to be networked electronically on the 1.5 metre grid mentioned earlier. Also

since some universities involve private sector funding and are a risk investment, there is always the possibility that general teaching space will be adapted to lettable offices in the future. Hence, the market standard for commercial space is a useful benchmark for universities to follow.

Frequently, the 13–15 metre width is adopted for two parallel wings divided by a central atrium-like street running through the centre. The 'street' can contain social facilities (cafes, shops etc) which animate the space and give it an internal version of Jefferson's lawn at the University of Virginia. The street becomes a place of student rendezvous, of discussion

11.3   Aerial view, new campus, University of Nottingham, UK, by Michael Hopkins and Partners.

and contact between staff and scholars. This is the format adopted at the Royal Docks Campus, University of East London in the Docklands. The masterplan was prepared in 1994 by RMJM with the detailed design undertaken in 1999 by Edward Cullinan and Partners. A central concourse gives access on either side to general teaching space and leads to shared facilities – library, health centre, lecture theatres and cinema – each designed as landmarks along the route.[1] At the end of the 'street' or concourse stands the student village arranged as informal courtyards overlooking the water of Royal Dock.

The delineation between street and teaching space gives one further benefit, the concourse can perform as an environmental filter throughout the development. In the major expansion of the University of Nottingham by Michael Hopkins and Partners, the internal streets and corridors act as air-conditioning ducts to distribute the air through the building by natural means. The corridors and stair towers are a distribution network for circulating air throughout the development using the simple expedient of the solar stack effect, augmented on still days by extract fans. Windows allow fresh air into the building which as it heats rises to the stair

towers using corridors, concourses and atria to encourage movement. The shallow-plan teaching block is simple and repetitive in layout to allow the building to achieve energy economies over more traditional solutions of 75 per cent.[2] A large wind cowl at the top of each stair tower helps to extract the stale air and solar panels are used to drive the electric motors in the fans.

Four Case Studies of General Teaching Space

(a)   *Business School, Reading University, UK*

Designed by Rick Mather, the brief for this new business school (1998) was for a 'building of a quality one would expect in the City with some of the atmosphere of a dealing room'.[3] The client wanted a signature building both as a means of attracting students in the competitive world of postgraduate business studies and as a way of landmarking one of the entrances to the campus. A character of transparency and accessibility pervades the design – academic staff have glass-walled offices, there is an avoidance of corridors in favour of

11.4　Plan (first floor left, ground floor right) Business School, Reading University, UK, by Rick Mather.

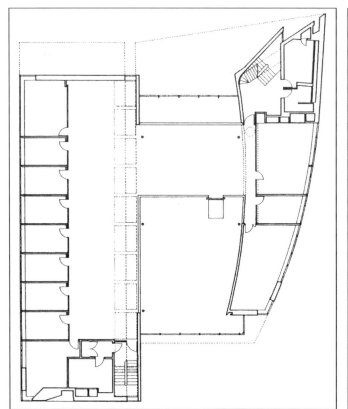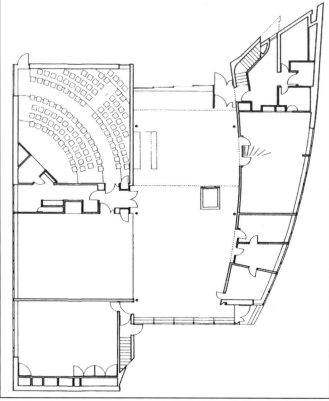

wide teaching or research space – with the result that the feeling of an academic warren is avoided.[4]

The building provides four elements of accommodation each designed to encourage the mixing of scholars, staff and visitors. A simulated computerised dealing room acts as a market place of learning, there is a large seminar room accessed from the cafe above, and an open deck of a reading room provides a bridge between offices and formal teaching. The PhD students occupy another open-planned area on the upper floor lined on one side by academics housed in their glass offices and on the other by a further balcony overlooking the common area. The strategy is one of interaction with the architecture deliberately creating links, both real and metaphorical, in the building. Only the leture theatre is fully enclosed and sealed from the

outside world, and its presence is signalled externally by a projecting soffit of raked seats.

The planning of the building sets up two conditions which are then separated by a double-height central space. The first is a two-storey rectangular block of offices, meeting rooms and PhD space. The second is the bespoke collection of resource centre and seminar rooms whose outer edge follows the curving line of the perimeter road to the campus. Between the two is the double-height informal teaching and cafe space which also acts as a grand entrance lobby for the business school.

Mather has met a demanding brief by adapting the geometry of campus alignment and the specific quality of business studies to create a landmark. In particular, the architect has studied how space is used in acad-

11.5 Plan, Business School and Economics Building, Loughborough University, UK, by Ahrends, Burton and Koralek.

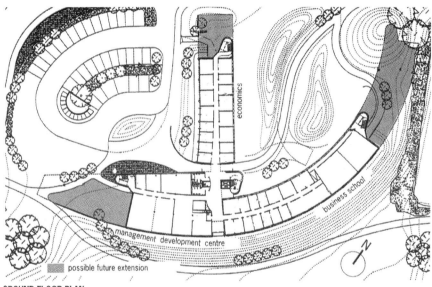

GROUND FLOOR PLAN

emia and in business, and has drawn some fresh conclusions. He was encouraged by the brief to exploit interior space as the medium of learning as against the usual assumption in favour of enclosed offices. As a result nearly 70 per cent of the new business school is free flowing space in one form or another. And where enclosure occurs it is normally via storey-height glass walls, not plastered blockwork partitions which are the usual pattern. As a result this is a transparent, luminous container of learning – providing a welcoming and lively environment and an interesting gateway to the campus.

Building	Architect	Special Features	Cost
Business School, Reading University	Rick Mather	• Signature building to attract best students and academics	£1.8 million
		• Quasi-dealing room as teaching space	
		• Emphasis upon open plan, not celular accommodation	
		• Use of glass walls to provide visual interaction	

(b)   Business School and Economics Building, Loughborough University, UK

Designed by Ahrends, Burton and Koralek, the new business and economics building at Loughborough

University (1997) is a three-storey sweeping terrace of teaching accommodation which helps complete the campus masterplan. Sitting alongside a public road to the east of the university it edges the sports fields nearby while forming a new landmark and gateway to the campus. The building shape is simple: a crescent of accommodation for the business school with a stem at right angles for the economics department. Both arms of the building can be extended outwards, providing the opportunity for future growth.

The plan provides the necessary balance of teaching, seminar, research and staff rooms with little fuss. The form is driven by a combination of environmental and operational factors. The plan depth of 15 metres allows for effective low-energy design while also enhancing buildability and giving the optimum structural frame dimensions for functional change. A central corridor is employed, edged to one side by structural columns at 6-metre centres. Flexible partitions allow a combination of cellular office and open teaching areas to be formed as demand dictates with only the stairs, lifts and entrance foyer designed as permanent parts. Since

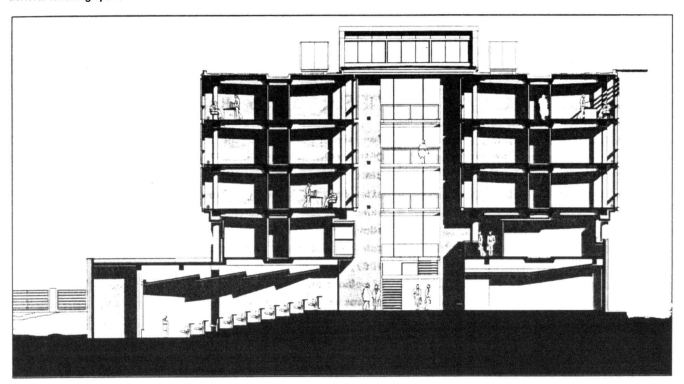

11.6 Section, School of Management, UMIST, Manchester, UK, by ORMS Architects.

the two departments share a common entrance, the public areas have a higher level of investment than faculty teaching areas. This is evident particularly in the entrance foyer where curving walls give the internal lobby a sense of occasion.

The plan successfully unites building and landscape at a campus level and also at the detailed grain of arrival. The central arm successfully divides pedestrians from vehicles but all visitors converge in a small square before arrival. This sense of 'threshold' is a feature of the building: contemplative space is provided at the main functional divisions between public and private accommodation as well as at the interface between outside and inside.[5] The latter reaches a climax in the three-storey entrance hall

Building	Architect	Special Features	Cost
Business School and Economics Building, Loughborough University, UK	Ahrends, Burton and Koralek	• Crescent shape which forms edge to campus	£744/ m^2
		• Wings which can be extended	
		• Narrow plan depth for energy efficiency	
		• Clever segregation of pedestrians and vehicles at entrance	

which is crossed at high level by bridges linking the two departments.

The rational and the particular both find expression in the building. From the outside the window grid and structural columns allude to the repetitive nature of interior accommodation. The curving footprint, however, relates to the campus plan and the position of older neighbours. The projecting stairs at the end of each wing provide sculptural terminations, an effect enhanced by cubic set backs on the upper floors. Although a loss of detailed quality may have resulted from the 'design and build' procurement path adopted by the university[6], this building confirms the thesis that every building on campus has dual duty – to enrich the whole and to provide useful operational accommodation.

(c)   School of Management, University of Manchester Institute of Science and Technology (UMIST), UK

The Manchester School of Management at UMIST (1997) designed by ORMS Architects consists of three floors of cellular offices placed above lecture theatres and general teaching space on the lower two floors. A large central atrium provides a social centre to the School while enhancing daylight levels in the core of the building. The atrium runs through the full height of the block, and being generously proportioned, provides repose and tranquility in the very heart of the business school. On either side of

130

11.7   Plans, Judge Institute of Management Studies, Cambridge University, UK, by John Outram and Partners.

Building	Architect	Special Features	Cost
School of Management, UMIST	ORMS Architects	• Rational plan based upon comercial office design • Atrium in centre to form enviromental and social space • Extensive use of cellular offices	£900/m^2

the atrium are double banked offices with their own central corridor with the raked lecture theatres on the ground floor set partly into the ground to avoid disrupting the order of the cross section.

This is a rational linear building. It does not attempt to create a landmark to the campus: it quietly performs its function of providing efficient, flexible teaching space. The elevations reflect directly the plan and section, with an orthogonal grid ordering every part. In basic form there is much similarity to Rab Bennett's innovative PowerGen Building near Coventry, even down to the use of expressed concrete ceiling coffers as environmental moderators. But the Manchester School of Business building is air-conditioned, not naturally ventilated as in Bennett's case, and the permitted cost levels (at £900 per m^2) are less than modern commercial office standards.[7]

The building raises one important question: how far should the need for private office space by academics dictate the plan? When so much of business thrives on open plan or group working, how can separate cellular offices be justified in the university sector. This is particularly true for a business school which, in theory at least, learns from the world of work. There are cost implications for the private academic office which can undermine the provision of more lasting features of a building, such as teaching space, finishes in the public areas and level of provision for students.

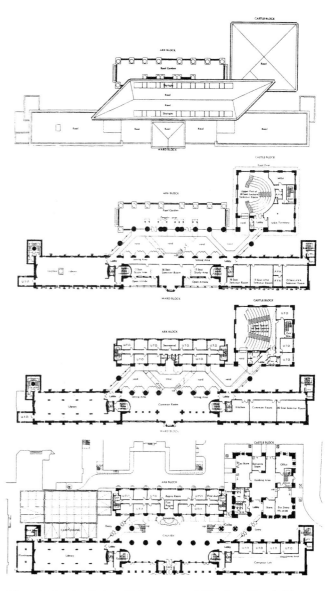

(d)   *Judge Institute of Management Studies, Cambridge University, UK*

Designed by John Outram, the Judge Institute (1994) is a new centre for business and management studies at Cambridge University. The building breaks with current practice: it is a large postmodern classical building which has a powerful order of almost Byzantine proportions. Whereas teaching buildings elsewhere provide neutral, flexible space, the Judge Institute asserts a unifying historicist presence upon all the accommodation – offices, seminar rooms, library and lecture theatre.

Outram's design owes its justification to two influences: the presence of an adjoining nineteenth-century former hospital to which it is physically linked, and Outram's preference, supported by the client, for an architectural ritual which gives dignity to university education. The architect has arguably done as much to transform the former hospital as to create new accommodation behind. The centre of the old ward block forms the new entrance to the Management Institute with an extra storey added, and the square in front facing Trumpington Street has been formalised. An open gallery now constitutes the entrance with library and computer laboratory slotted into the outer wings of the ward block. Behind is a four-storey bank of new offices with a large lecture theatre to one side.

The section is more complex than the plan. Between the converted hospital block and the new bank of staff offices sits a lofty, open, temple-like atrium. It is a shared space for meeting, a forum which divides old from new, and places the whole beneath a dramatic polychrome of construction materials and applied paint. The classical overtures of this space owe something to nineteenth-century architects, such as Alexander Thomson in Glasgow, and are justified by Outram as the need to create a temple for ideas.[8] Walkways and diagonal bridges criss-cross the space, exposing the interior to close scrutiny.

Beneath the obvious post-modernity of detail there exists a logic which owes something to Louis Kahn's concept of expressed service towers (eg Richards Medical Research Building, Philadelphia) and something to the local Cambridge context. For whereas Kahn provides intellectual support for the idea of a horizontal and vertical articulation based upon the

Building	Architect	Special Features	Cost
Judge Institute, Cambridge University	John Outram and Partners	• Post-modern classical design	Not available
		• Columns used as service ducts	
		• Makes reference to 'Cambridge' classical tradition	
		• Uses existing building to inform architectural order	

dictates of building services, Downing College and Quinlan Terry's nearby library create a powerful immediate neighbourhood of classically inspired architecture. What Outram does is to join them together to create a building which is both modern and ancient, inviting yet exclusive, with ideas about colour and space which challenge orthodoxy. That, afterall, is what Cambridge has always striven for in its university architecture. Modernity in Cambridge is normally the result of looking backwards.

Notes

1. RMJM Project Note, 'Royals University College Campus', 1995.
2. Will Callaghan, 'Building for the Future', *The Guardian,* 29 June 1999, p 9.
3. Robert Bevan, 'Business Class', *Building Design,* 12 March 1999, p 15.
4. Ibid.
5. Peter Fawcett, 'Building Economy', *The Architects' Journal,* 18 June 1998, p 31.
6. Ibid, p 32.
7. Frank Duffy, 'Managing a Miracle', *RIBA Journal,* October 1998, p 41.
8. *Architecture Today,* AT 63, November 1995, p 49.

Student housing

Halls of residence form the background architecture to many campuses: they are the more sober and neutral buildings against which the campus landmarks (library, sports hall etc) are set. Universities vary a great deal in character. Some are highly residential in character, others assume that most students will live off campus. With cuts in student maintenance grants, the trend today is towards students living at home and commuting on a daily basis to their local university.

However, it is still commonplace for all first year students and at some universities for all undergraduates to be housed in specially provided halls of residence. As long ago as 1970 the UK University Grants Committee warned that a shortage of residential accommodation could become the biggest single bottleneck in the expansion of higher education[1]. Living away from home is seen by many as part of the 'university experience' and action by government in the provision of higher education has largely been to promote an environment of learning in the broadest sense. Student housing is, therefore, needed to manage the transition away from home. Halls of residence allow the university to provide a supportive environment which protects students from the harshness and expense of the private rental sector. Campus housing ensures too that individual students have a sense of community in which to belong, one which fosters study and social interaction as against the isolation, depression and boredom of bedsits.

Most universities offer a varied range of student housing in order to provide choice between type, standard and cost. A wide portfolio of provision allows the university to take advantage of the conference market when students are not on campus, and to attract different types of student (married, single parent, disabled). Such flexibility leads to variety of built form which can give the campus greater richness of environment than with single housing types. Since student housing needs to be self-funded (ie without government grants) variety of provision can reduce financial risk in a world of educational change.

It is common for universities to plan to house 40 per cent of their student population in halls of residence and

12.1 Sketch, St John's College, Oxford University, UK, by MacCormac, Jamieson Prichard.

12.2 Halls of residence, University of California, Davis, USA.

perhaps as many as 5 per cent of their academic staff. Integration of students and staff in halls helps promote responsible behaviour and build a collegiate spirit. In certain types of accommodation the close interaction of staff and students is part of the management of the hall. Certainly accommodation is needed for newly appointed staff, visiting lecturers and external examiners. Specific accommodation is also provided for married students and those with disabilities even where an obligation to house all students is not undertaken. As a result housing represents in volume terms the largest single capital invest-ment among the various types of building on a typical campus.[2] Like housing in the city, halls of residence are the essential backcloth to university life both socially and architecturally.

Most students are young, single and adaptable but some have special needs. The integration of types of student (young and mature, single and married, able and disabled) helps development socially and educationally. Hence with-in a typical hall of residence a variety of accommodation may

be needed. Generally speaking student accommodation needs to provide:

- a residential environment which supports study as well as recreation
- privacy and quiet within 'family' or social units of about six to eight students
- opportunities for informal academic discourse
- a safe and secure environment, inside and out.

Student housing is not usually profitable but it is recog-nised that poor residential provision for the student makes learning difficult. Private residences and students living at home increase the gulf between curricula and extra-curricula life, to the detriment of the university experience. The Oxbridge pattern of residential college where students and faculty staff share a common life is one extreme and the com-muting student studying from the parents' home another. Between the two lies the modern provision of student hous-ing whether in nine-storey slab blocks, as designed at Berkeley by Walter Gropius, or Alvar Aalto's more informal housing crescents at MIT. The dormitory system with class-rooms on one floor and bedrooms above, popular earlier in the century on campuses in the USA and in Germany, is currently out of favour. But whatever system of student housing provision is adopted, it is vital that residential

12.3   Various plan types for student housing at Buckinghamshire, Chilterns University College, Buckingham, UK, by Corrigan, Soundy, Kilaiditi Associates.

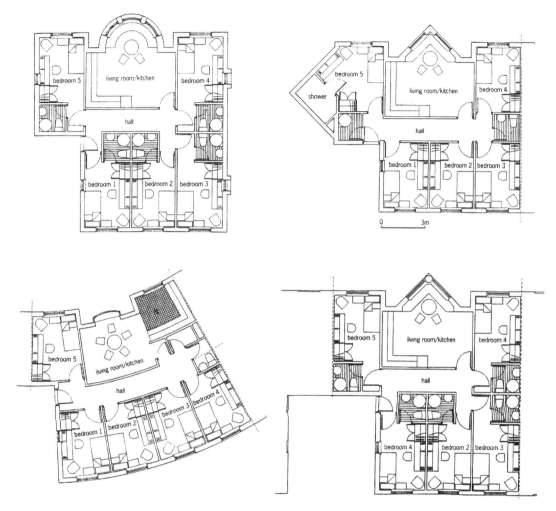

12.4   Plan, student residences, St John's College, Oxford University, UK, by MacCormac, Jamieson Prichard.

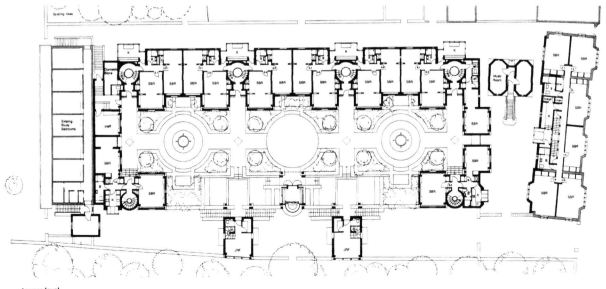

terrace level

12.5   Queen Mary and Westfield College, London, student housing by MacCormac, Jamieson Prichard.

accommodation does not lag behind other forms of construction on campus. It is a measure of the health of a university that the student experience outside the classroom is given proper attention. Students on campus value the shared purpose of university life but often resent the sense of living in an institutional environment.[3] Hence, the type of hall or hostel system adopted and its uniqueness of design impacts directly upon student perceptions.

Housing types

Halls of residence come in many forms depending upon the ethos of the university. There are three main types of university hall either built on campus or in a separate student village:

• collegiate halls with integral dining, recreational facilities and some teaching facilities

• dense blocks of study bedrooms with shared laundry and dining facilities
• small groups of study bedrooms revolving around informal kitchen and dining areas.

Not all universities employ a single type, many such as York and Warwick in the UK or University of California, Davis, use a combination of approaches and even at universities such as Cambridge and Princeton, which traditionally employed collegiate halls, the modern pattern is towards self-catering residential halls. It is a trend which recognises the need to provide not just accommodation but units of living and study which reinforce the sense of cohesive social groups.

Students are rarely invited to comment upon the type and standard of accommodation they would prefer. However, surveys of student opinion suggest that the main concerns are rent levels and value for money, safety and security, access, room size and facilities (including private bathrooms) and noise transmission levels.[4] The latter is a particular problem where rooms are designed for leisure, study and sleep. Noise too is a source of complaint with vocational courses (such as medicine, nursing or hotel catering) where practice–based study requires sleep during the day.

The architectural typology of student housing varies markedly. The collegiate hall is invariably a courtyard of accommodation, sometimes directly linked to a library or lecture theatre. Here student bedrooms and staff offices are closely integrated (as at Canterbury) with dining and common rooms providing formal punctuation. In the past the collegiate hall was single sex but today mixed sex provision is more common. Similarly the pattern of student and master has given way to greater emphasis upon student autonomy. In spite of recent changes, the collegiate hall of residence balances student freedom with institutional control over behaviour. As a type the collegiate hall has the benefit of being instantly recognisable, and of projecting through built form the philosophy and identity of the university.

In addition, the collegiate hall fosters a sense of belonging to a small unit as against a large university. The integral nature of collegiate halls engenders loyalty to a community, support for personal development, and provides a learning environment separate from that of the students' faculty. Halls, therefore, exist as satellites slightly separate from the mainstream of university activity, yet benefiting from proximity to the main campus facilities.

Alternatively, study bedrooms can be arranged as repetitive units within large dense blocks. This pattern, not unlike a hotel, has economy of scale, cost and maintenance. Students here share dining, recreational, social and laundry facilities, either on the ground floor or at intermediate floors within the building. Such blocks are frequently fairly tall (14 storey residential towers at Essex University housing 200 study bedrooms) or arranged as linear halls of residence (Rootes Hall, Warwick University with each block housing 500 students). Both patterns have the advantage of ensuring close proximity between the living and learning environments, but at a cost to campus character and social cohesion. Where high rise halls of residence are employed they do, however, help preserve the quality of the external landscape which can be planted as parkland. The views too can be impressive and conducive to reflective thought.

Repetition allows prefabrication to be employed which, in theory at least, drives down building costs and makes replacement of damaged parts easier. System construction is often speedier than traditional building methods and with the construction of new universities, this can be a benefit. Whether high rise or linear, large repetitive blocks of student housing offer administrative advantages but few benefits to the students. The chance of casual encounter is not helped by the configuration of tall or linear blocks, certainly the scale leads to anonymity with the lift providing the main means of social exchange. Noise too can be a problem, as can uni-

12.6 Collegiate atmosphere at St John's College, Oxford University, UK, by MacCormac, Jamieson Prichard.

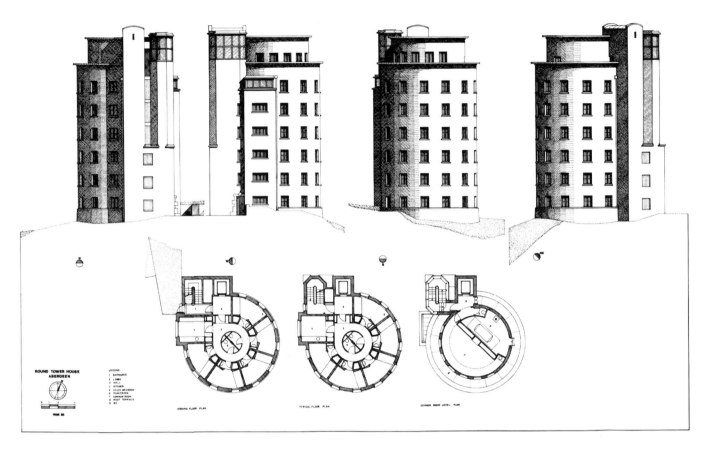

12.7 Student housing, Robert Gordon University, Aberdeen, UK, by Jeremy Dixon, Edward Jones.

12.8 Erdman Hall Dormitories, student housing in linked towers, by Louis Kahn (1960), Bryn Mawr College, Pennsylvania, USA.

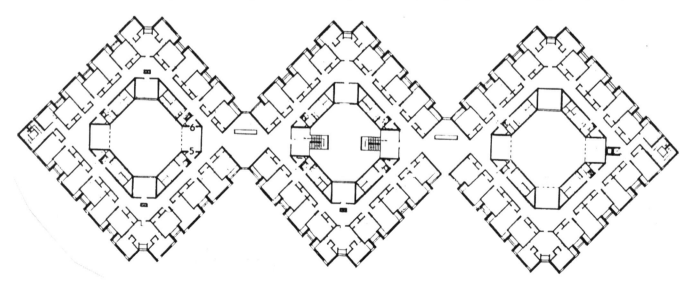

formity of internal and external treatment, and for visitors or parents, the impressive can be one of overcrowding.

The third common type of student residence is the block of small groups of study bedrooms which share a kitchen and dining area. Usually up to four storeys high the arrangement is akin more to an apartment block than a hotel. Normally about 8 students form a living module, each with their own room which gives direct access to a kitchen (with washing machine and dryer) and small eating area. This type of layout is today the most common form of student housing in Europe and combines benefits of the collegiate and dense block layouts. The small compact blocks, perhaps consisting of three or four modules stacked vertically, are sometimes self-contained or arranged as linear terraces (eg.

12.9 Student housing in long south-facing blocks for energy efficiency. Strathclyde University, Glasgow, UK, by GRM Kennedy and Partners with Kaiser Bautechnik.

Solar Residences at University of Strathclyde, Constable Terrace at University of East Anglia or Storthes Hall, University of Huddersfield).

As a general rule college halls provide central catering, with hostels and flat units self-catering. However, even in traditional halls of residence a degree of self catering is required (either in the student room or in a shared kitchen). Students in self-catering houses also have access to central catering facilities on the main campus. So catering provision is not normally the generator of the type of student housing but once the form of student residences is decided it is important that an appropriate catering strategy is evolved.

Whichever of the three typologies (collegiate, dense blocks, social units) is adopted, it is vital that students should have their own study bedroom. As its name implies this is a bedroom with purpose built study desk, a campus connection for personal computer, space for books and a filing cabinet. A high level of sound insulation between rooms and rooms and corridors is needed. The facility should exist also to allow the student to moderate the internal temperature, by opening windows and adjusting blinds. The trend towards central environmental control in the inter-

ests of energy efficiency should be balanced by a degree of student choice. This helps to alleviate stress and depression which are common features of undergraduate life.

Funding and flexibility

Most student housing is today privately financed using a capital loan and interest repayments rather akin to a mortgage. Government grants for student housing in the UK ceased in 1974 and world-wide the pattern is of loan-financed schemes rather than direct grant. Some well-endowed universities can draw upon private capital or direct grants from companies or individuals but most are subject to normal market forces. Since universities are long lived institutions there is little risk in providing student housing as long as initial costs are kept under control, the design is relatively maintenance free, and as long as some flexibility is provided. The latter is to allow the buildings to change the nature of their provision over time by, for example permitting the university to benefit from summer lettings (perhaps to tourists, business people or families) when students are not on campus.

As a typical student tenancy in a hall of residence is 35 weeks, the university is under pressure to generate an

12.10 Student housing, Robert Gordon University, Aberdeen, UK, by Jeremy Dixon, Edward Jones.

children. Hence some flexibility in layout is needed if the business or tourist tenant is to be attracted. Most student rooms have single beds and no en-suite bathroom facilities. Where summer lets are to be maximised it makes sense to provide some limited form of *en suite* toilet facilities. The provision of linking rooms internally to form a larger family-sized apartment also makes sense by the use of lockable folding partitions or doors. In the design of student housing it is prudent, therefore, to consider the needs of other potential tenants by providing occupational flexibility initially.

The rigours of funding normally result in some kind of 'design and build' contract for halls of residence. The repetitive nature of student housing favours the involvement of contractors in the procurement process. Architectural design is still needed but when student bed spaces of two to three thousand are required (as in a typical new university) the economies of design and build prevail. As a process 'design and build', or 'design and management' contracts using a project manager employed directly by the university, offers speed, cost and quality control advantages. But design innovation and quality of image may suffer in

income from the remaining 17 weeks. Most exploit the summer vacation by running summer schools and conferences or make student rooms available for holiday lets. As many universities are located in tourist locations (York, Edinburgh, Lincoln and Oxford in the UK; San Francisco, New York and Seattle in the USA; Paris, Lyon and Bordeaux in France) there is little problem in secondary lettings.

However, accommodation suitable for a single student is rarely appropriate for a holiday couple or family with

12.11 Interior, student room, Balliol College, Oxford University, UK, by MacCormac, Jamieson Prichard.

the pursuit of efficiency. Since modern universities compete with each other to attract good students and staff, the added value of design uniqueness should not be overlooked.

Detail design

A typical undergraduate study bedroom is about 12 square metres and 14 square metres for postgraduate provision. Since the modern student is normally armed with a personal computer and a design student with a drawing board, the trend is towards slightly larger space standards than in the past. Much depends upon the type of student and the layout of accommodation. Some rooms contain space for a kettle or a small stove, others provide space merely for a bed, desk, wardrobe and window. A minimum room width of 2.5 metres is required with private bathrooms (if provided) helping with noise insulation between corridors and rooms.

Study bedrooms are arranged in four main configurations:

* linear corridor with double banked study bedrooms
* central staircase with perimeter study bedrooms
* lift core with perimeter study bedrooms
* corridors, stairs or lifts serving student 'houses'.

The first is limited by consideration of fire escape, and anonymity of character. The second by climbing height (usually four storeys), the third by lift capacity and noise, the fourth by sociability (or disturbance). Irrespective of the room arrangement, the designer needs to create an independent character for units of accommodation rather than the sense of institutional sameness. Normally a group of study bedrooms form a 'family' or 'household' unit which shares kitchen, eating, laundry facilities and TV facilities. As a general rule between six and twenty-four bedrooms share common living room facilities with the norm about eight to twelve. In collegiate accommodation the 'family' unit tends to be larger because of the presence of college based dining accommodation. In large dense housing blocks the families are smaller in order to create a sense of belonging. The 'family' or 'household' unit is essentially a social group-

ing for students of roughly similar age and aspiration. Normally each unit has its own locked door which leads via a hall to locked bedroom doors and the unlocked communal facilities. In management terms one student acts as leader of the unit liaising with management services (cleaning, security etc) for the whole building and sometimes with policing for the whole campus.

The kitchen/dining area is a social focus for the student household, a place to cook an omelette and to throw a party. To help build a sense of community in this type of accommodation, the pattern is one of increasing the size of shared self-catering facilities and proportionally reducing the area of study bedrooms. As communal accommodation increases in size, the need for noise insulation grows in importance. Noise is a common source of friction in student households and sleep disturbance due to excessive noise can be cited as a reason for poor examination performance. It is consequently in the university's interest not to neglect the importance of sound insulation when design briefs are being prepared.

In the USA it is commonplace for student rooms on campus to have a wash-basin and sometimes also a shower and WC. In the UK provision normally stops at the hand-basin. The decision as whether to provide *en suite* facilities is determined partly by expectations of non-student letting (over the summer vacation) and partly by the layout. If toilets are located nearby the case for *en suite* is undermined but with over twelve students sharing a communal bathroom the argument for providing facilities within rooms becomes stronger. Also, if the hall of residence is for postgraduates and perhaps visiting scholars from other countries, *en suite* toilets become imperative.

As sound is such a problem in densely occupied student halls, the materials which form the finishes need to address noise abatement. Wall-to-wall carpeting (in rooms and corridors), acoustic tiles and hessian wall finishes greatly help with sound absorption as does the use of soft furnishings. Normally sound insulation of 45 dB is required between rooms. Particular attention to noise abatement is needed around lifts, telephones and with self-closing door systems.

Students like to personalise their rooms so the bedroom design needs to provide flexibility for different furniture

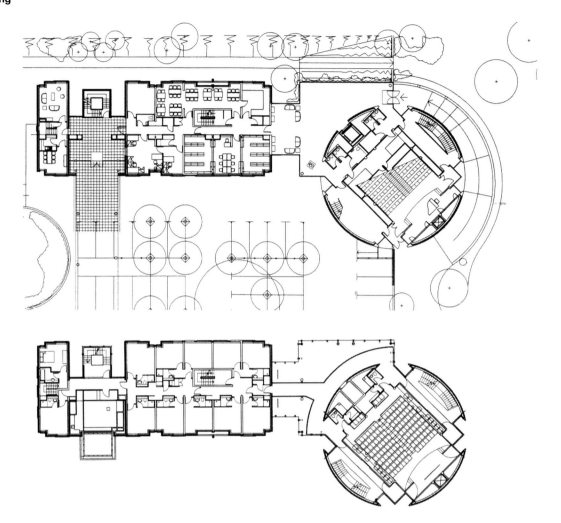

12.12   Plan (ground floor above, typical upper floor below), Kaetsu College, Cambridge University, UK, by Austin: Smith-Lord.

layouts and durability of finish. Wall space is also needed for posters and many socket outlets obviously encourage a variety of styles of occupation. Since space is at a premium the area beneath beds and above built-in wardrobes is often employed for storage. As student needs differ, the size of rooms can vary within a household unit. Some students may be willing to pay higher rents for extra space or amenities, and variation supports the idea of diversity of provision for different types or ages of student.

Three Case Studies of Student Housing in the College Tradition

(a)   Kaetsu College, Cambridge University, UK

Kaetsu College (1995) is a small Japanese foundation associated with Cambridge University. It follows the Oxbridge pattern of being an integrated development of student residences, dining room, college library and lecture theatre, arranged as a courtyard alongside older neighbours. The design by architects Austin: Smith-Lord extends New Hall, developed in 1960 as a model of pro-

gressive college architecture, into a composition drawing upon the educational traditions of Europe and Asia.

Kaetsu College borrows many concepts from New Hall described at the time as a 'serious plan ... allied to formal inventiveness'[5]. At Kaetsu, as at New Hall, the arrangement consists of residential wings enclosing well planted gardens with shared facilities (in New Hall's case the college library) providing a point of sculptural punctuation to the composition. The rotunda lecture theatre at Kaetsu College acts as an entrance to the whole development and provides a point of visual reference when viewing the new college from Huntingdon Road. Being circular it refers to the rotunda of New Hall's library and to ancient college architecture, but by adopting a modern and transparent architectural style the references are obliquely to the globalisation of higher education.

The new college blends east with west. There is an undeniable hint of Japan in the detailing of fenestration and approach to planting design, a sense heightened by a ceremonial tea garden on an upper

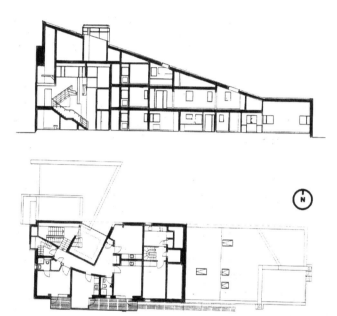

12.13 Section and plan, Pippard House, Clare College, Cambridge University, UK, by Nicholas Ray Associates.

Building	Architect	Special Features	Cost
Kaetsu College, Cambridge	Austin:Smith-Lord	• Blends English and Japanese traditions • Modernises the typology of the Cambridge College • Uses lecture theatre as gateway	£2,196/m^2

floor terrace. But the arrangement of college rooms in the residential wing follows orthodoxy, except that each study bedroom has an *en suite* bathroom, and stairs are placed externally to provide well-lit architectural movement spaces. Also where bedroom doors occur the corridor space is widened to form a small internal court for casual gossip.

Kaetsu College is a self-contained residential college for Japanese scholars visiting Cambridge. There is everything a visitor may require in dignified, well detailed residential surroundings. The integration of study, lecture, ritual and residential facilities in a single development helps give the College greater architectural interest than in a hall of purely residential character. It evokes well the traditional mood of a Cambridge college with its courts, wings of study bedrooms and landmarking lecture theatre. Perhaps the greatest single element in the success of the building is the way stairs, lifts and corridors have been given a central place in the drama of the building. Routes to and through the College are celebrations of passage, encouraging contemplation and reflection upon university life.[6]

(b) Pippard House, Clare College, Cambridge University, UK

Pippard House (1996), designed by Nicholas Ray Associates, is similar to the Princeton Institute for Advanced Studies, a postgraduate community of scholars and senior visiting academics.[7] It is a mainly residential graduate college, with specific accommodation for families as well as single students, and provides a large communal dining room in addition to private living/dining areas in each apartment.

The building balances well the dual needs of privacy and communality in a student hall of residence. With £30,000 per room available the budget allowed for greater architectural enterprise than is normally found in college halls. The plan and section encourage interaction through the medium not only of large common rooms and dining areas but in the broad curving corridors and dwelling space alongside the lifts. The section rises to three storeys towards the west providing the penetration of afternoon sunlight into the main stairs of the building. The sloping section gives two further benefits: it allows a combination of single rooms and double height flats to be constructed in the same shell, and it maintains a link with Ralph Erskine's earlier buildings of 1966 for Clare College. These too established a domes-

12.14 Halls of residence, Balliol College, Oxford University, UK, by MacCormac, Jamieson Prichard.

Building	Architect	Special Features	Cost
Pippard House, Clare College, Cambridge	Nicholas Ray Associates	• Mixed single students and family accommadation	£30,000 per student room
		• Large shared dining/ common rooms to encourage academic exchange	
		• Sloping section to provide complexity and external views	
		• Provision of niches for quiet reflection	

(c)   Halls of Residence, Balliol College, Oxford University, UK

tic vocabulary which allowed the interior accommodation to penetrate the enclosing walls, creating in the process delicate cantilevered balconies beneath crisply angled roofs.

In providing graduate accommodation of various types, Pippard House responds to the complexity of the brief by exploiting twists in plan as well as angles in section. The result is a group of buildings for eighty students which have informal semi-private gardens and alleyways between them. These spaces contrast with the expansive open prospect to the rugby ground nearby. Views are exploited at every opportunity, via balconies and niches, slots in plan and a lantern roof light which brings the sky unexpectedly into play.

The various architectural incidents encourage the mind to wander. The building engages in the poetics of space in a fashion which hints at the complexity of academic discourse. Order here is skilfully broken down to display the unexpected and to give validity in brick and concrete to disorder. In this the scholar may seek some comfort and inspiration.

The new halls of residence (1998) at Balliol College, Oxford, designed by MacCormac Jamieson Prichard, break with the tradition of the courtyard college and form instead a linear terrace running alongside the college sports field. The halls are arranged as small towers, four-storeys high with three levels of student accommodation above lecture theatres, formal dining areas and staff flats. The residential floors consist of six to eight study bedrooms sharing a kitchen, making a total of twenty-one students in each tower. The towers are organised around a central stair and are linked together via an internal corridor

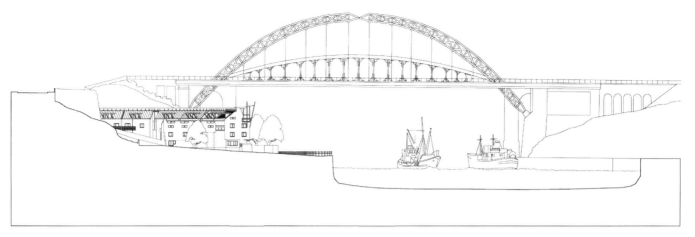

12.15 Site section, student housing, Panns Bank, University of Sunderland, UK, by Feilden Clegg Architects.

Building	Architect	Special Features	Cost
News Halls of, Residence, Balliol College, Oxford	MacCormac, Jamieson Prichard	• Informal grouping of small towers • Accidental encounter spaces • Available for conferences	£1,224/ m²

and bridge which has views outwards on opposite sides. The lower level lecture theatre and public areas spill out into the adjoining landscape, creating an opposing character to the secure and inward world of the student rooms above.

The design exploits the benefits of accidental encounter. Rooms have diagonally placed windows to catch glimpses of the internal courtyard between adjoining blocks, and there is much use made of window seats, meeting spaces in corridors, and lounge areas placed on stair landings. The inspiration for this is Christopher Alexander's book The *Pattern Language* (1968) with its advocation of small-scaled social interaction space at the thresholds of functional change. The shared kitchen acts as the main anchor for student interaction on the upper floors, the lecture theatre for students and public on the ground floor. Designed for conference use, the standard and cost of construction is higher than the norm, but the Balliol tradition of architectural solidity and complexity has been maintained by thoughtful design.[8]

Two Case Studies of Low-Energy Student Housing

(a) Panns Bank, University of Sunderland, UK

The main interest in the Panns Bank student residences (1994) at the University of Sunderland lies in

the creation of energy-efficient housing which exploits solar design principles in a location in the relatively sunless north of England.[9] The buildings, three-storeys high with further accommodation in the roofspace, cater for 276 students who pay for their own electricity consumption via localised meters in each study bedroom. The latter is an attempt to distinguish between rent and energy consumption in order to motivate students to conserve fuel.

Many features combine to make this a model of low-energy student residences: besides exploiting passive solar design for space heating and natural ventilation, the blocks have high levels of fabric insulation, the construction is well sealed, and low-energy lighting is employed throughout. Heating and hot water is controlled via a building energy management system (BEMS) with mechanical ventilation reserved for bathrooms and kitchens.

The design by Feilden Clegg is based upon the normal pattern of six students forming a self-contained house sharing kitchen, living spaces and bathroom facilities. The blocks are orientated to the south, arranged in shallow curves facing onto landscaped courts. To avoid summer overheating there is a large projecting eaves canopy and balconies are employed to shade windows on lower storeys. The plan places the bulk of the study bedrooms on the south side with kitchen, bathrooms and staircases to the north.

Although construction costs at £16,400 per student were about 5 per cent above the norm for student housing, annual energy savings are around 18 per cent, giving a payback period of under ten years. However, while the savings flow mainly in the direction of lower student rents, the benefits have proved a useful marketing tool for the university, enhancing its image with the business community.

The development is part of a wider scheme of urban regeneration for the redundant shipyards along the River Wear. The curve of the riverside is part of

12.16 Low-energy student housing at Constable Terrace, University of East Anglia, Norwich, UK, designed by Rick Mather.

Building	Architect	Special Features	Cost
Student Housing, Panns Bank, University of Sunderland	Feilden Clegg	• Low-energy design • Nautical references for dockside site • Individual entrances • Separate room metering	£16,400 per student room (in 1994)

the justification for the serpentine lines employed in site planning. The layout exploits views over the water while also maximising passive solar gain from the southerly aspect. Part of the architectural language grows from reference to the former nautical use of the site. The external staircases, balconies and mast-like columns all stem from the shipyard tradition. They also help break down the institutional appearance of the scheme by giving groups of students their own private staircases to the flats.

(b)   Student Housing, Constable Terrace, University of East Anglia, Norwich, UK

The long snaking terrace of eight hundred student study bedrooms (1994) is the result of respect for

Foster Associates' nearby Sainsbury Centre (1978), a determination by campus planners to preserve a group of birch trees, and the requirements of low-energy design. Instead of designing a linear terrace, the architect Rick Mather adopted a curved form which flows effortlessly across the gentle sloping contours of the University of East Anglia. In order to avoid an institutional feel to a student residence of such size, the decision was made to group the rooms into 'houses' arranged as a traditional terrace. There are ten study bedrooms clustered into three-storey houses accessed by their own stair and front door and with their own ground-floor living room. Above them sits an independent floor of flatlets designed for staff or married students accessed via a central top-lit corridor.

It is a plan which was relatively economical to build because of the degree of repetition while at the same time proving to be highly energy efficient. Low-energy design was a feature of the brief and helped figure the site layout, plan, section and many of the building's details. The south facing terrace is highly insulated and air-tight, and to conserve energy further window openings are the minimum in area permitted under UK building law.[10] The building also employs a displacement ventilation system which draws in fresh air under the roof canopy and distributes it at low velocity to the study bedrooms. Mechanical ventilation in a student hall of residence is an unusual solution, yet

Building	Architect	Special Features	Cost
Constable Terrace, University of East Anglia	Rick Mather Architects	• Snake-like forms to preserve trees and respect site contours	£686/m^2 in 1994
		• Student flats as ten bedroom 'houses'	
		• Low-energy design	

it allows for the development of a smooth refined facade and clutter-free interiors. Added to this, external grilles above windows and the oversailing eaves, both required to avoid summertime over-heating, provide further architectural sophistication to the student hall of residence.

Notes

1. Tony Birks, *Building the New Universities,* David and Charles (1972), Newton Abbot, p 25.
2. Richard P Dober, *Campus, Planning,* Reinhold Publishing Corporation (1963), New York, p 119.
3. *New Metric Handbook,* Architectural Press (1999 edition), Oxford, p 341.
4. Ibid.
5. Michael Webb, 'Architecture in Britain Today', *Country Life,* 1968, p 20.
6. Brian Edwards, 'Squaring the Circle', *The Architects' Journal,* 19 September 1996, p 37.
7. Jeremy Melvin, 'Red Wedge', *RIBA Journal,* December 1997, p 39.
8. Isabel Allen, 'Continuous Assessment', *The Architects' Journal,* 11 February 1999, p 34.
9. *Energy Efficient Multi-Residential Accommodation: Panns Bank, University of Sunderland,* Initial Profile 91, Energy Efficiency Office (1995), London.
10. Mark Swenarton, 'Warm Space, Cool Aesthetic', *Architecture Today,* AT 45.30, February 1994.

Part three

Conclusions

CHAPTER 13

Why does the university campus matter?

Universities are 'places' as much as they are institutions. But they are not ordinary places: the campus is no business park or retail development, they are estates of buildings dedicated to higher learning. This has always been their role, and how they nurture the ideals of university education through the medium of architecture and urban design sets them apart from other building development.

Design ideals and innovative technologies

Taking a broad sweep of nearly a thousand years of university construction, it is possible to draw one significant

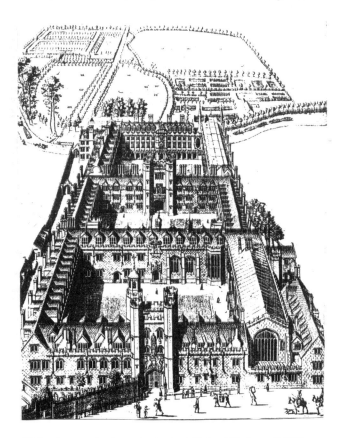

13.1   Loggan's view of a typical Oxford College (1675). Academic order reflected in university architecture.

13.2 As the problem of global warming was discovered by academics, it is no surprise to find universities exploiting low-energy design to develop a new aesthetic language. New Campus expansion at Nottingham University, UK, by Michael Hopkins and Partners.

conclusion. Of all building types none more conspicuously links new ideals of design and innovative technologies to the mission of development than the university. The exacting agendas of intellectual inquiry, of scientific experiment, and refined taste, are historically to be found in the design of many university buildings. For example, the sense of scientific rationalism is embodied in built form in the ancient universities of Oxford, Cambridge, Paris, Bolognia and Turin. The ideals of democracy find expression in the layout of universities from Virginia to Cape Town. In the present century, the expansion of universities to all sectors of society has seen the breaking down of physical and cultural walls, with many university buildings open to all and open all the time. The learning resource centre with its computer-based systems expresses both the cutting edge of information technology and the democratising of higher education. For these reasons the campus has never been an ordinary place.

The university is, therefore, a place of history, a microcosm in buildings and urban spaces which reflects the changing ideals of the world. Whereas it is frequently argued that this is true of the city at large, on the university campus ambition is higher, experiment more likely to be encouraged, and ideals more readily expressed. History teaches us so, and the present needs to keep this quality alive. Many of the case studies presented in this book demonstrate a continuing commitment to design innovation and in time these campus buildings will become another strand to our architectural or urban history.

The campus as a work of art

As an estate of buildings, sculpture, landscape and public spaces, the university is a work of art. Not readily perceived perhaps as high art, but representative of the human art of place making. The best ancient and modern campuses are 'places' not 'buildings'. They are enclosed, edged, centred, landmarked and memorable landscapes. The buildings are the backcloth to academic life: they contain functions but their content necessarily contributes to the pedagogic whole. Each building reflects the changing ideals of architecture, and the best today extend the debate,

13.3 Architectural experiment at the Sainsbury Centre, University of East Anglia, Norwich, UK, by Foster and Partners.

13.4 Architectural experiment at the Law Library, University of Cambridge, UK, by Foster and Partners.

The evolution of building types

Putting aside the great names of Western architecture, the campus is a good place to study the evolution of building types. The library, until the emergence of the public library around 1840, depended upon universities to evolve new forms of storing and using printed material. The development from the stall system to book cases and then open shelves in reading rooms, took place in the university library. Today, the emergence of the networked IT library has been led by universities, with city and national libraries following a few years behind. The same is true of the public auditorium which grew from the lecture theatre, or the science laboratory and the indoor sports hall. To some extent, too, the development of new forms of low-energy urban housing has grown from experiments conducted in the realm of student halls of residence.

Experiments in sustainable design

Nowhere is the sense of experiment and innovation greater than in the field of ecological design. Of all the most exciting projects under construction on the campuses across the world, the best are testing new forms of sustainable development. The reasons for this are obvious: the science of

pushing at the frontiers of taste or technology. The buildings by Rogers, Jourda and Foster described earlier do this, the masterplan for the expansion of the University of Nottingham by Hopkins adopts a similar ambition at a larger scale. The campus is, therefore, a work of art and a place for experiment.

Wren's contribution to the repertoire of university architecture is as great as that which he made to church design. Jefferson's visionary sense of landscape and urban design exceeds in the realm of campus making. Boullée, Latrobe and Schinkel all helped develop key campus building types. To understand architecture in all its complexity and invention there is no better concentration of built examples than on the typical university campus.

13.5 Thomas Slezer's view of Glasgow University (1690). Notice the college orchard and vegetable garden.

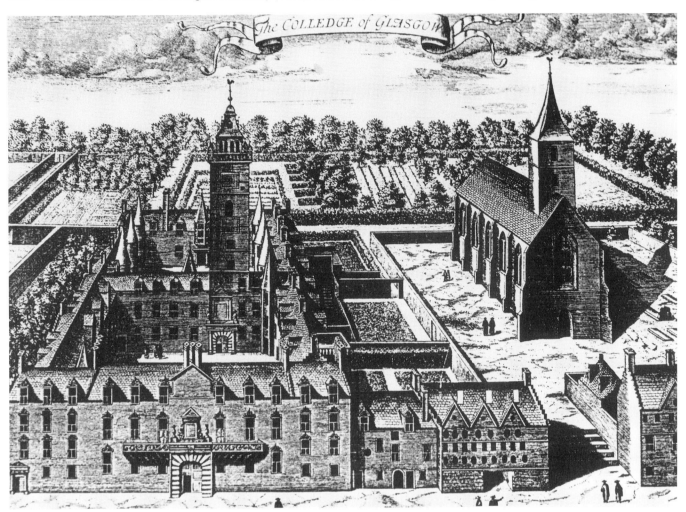

global warming emerged largely in universities, environmental concern spans academic boundaries and unites staff and students alike, and universities are less subject to the financial rigours of the market place than commercial developers. Sustainability has its origins in university research, and the best examples of how to fashion a more sustainable future are to be found in campus buildings around the world.

Ecological design has further advantages. By making a commitment to sustainability, the university is presenting an image of itself which has marketing advantages in terms of student recruitment. Green design improves the university's reputation with potential employers and the business community. When universities are in competition, image is important, and nothing expresses ideals more visibly than architecture. Green campus buildings pay in often invisible ways, by enhancing reputation, improving staff morale, creating landmarks, and in setting an example for the world at large to follow.

Ecological design, whether expressed in low-energy student housing or naturally ventilated and solar heated teaching space, allows buildings to be used as part of the pedagogic experience. Students can monitor performance, and, as at the University of East Anglia, benefit directly from the lower electricity bills, while staff can test their research ideas through the medium of building. Buildings not only express cultural ideals, they embody the laws of physics and environmental sciences. They make, therefore, good subjects to learn from and should be designed to demonstrate the great challenges of the day. This is the argument behind the Queen's Building at De Monfort University in Leicester, the Hamlyn Library at Thames Valley University, student housing at the University of Sunderland, and the design of the new science faculty at the University of Cyprus.

If the late-twentieth century campus seeks to embody the emerging discipline (as at Davis, UC) of sustainable development, sustainability has perhaps been a recurring theme over centuries. Many ancient universities contained orchards, herb and physics gardens, and, as at St Andrews in Scotland, dovecots for harvesting pigeons for the college table. These colleges were sustainable foundations, self-sufficient utopian communities which produced their own food and grew wherever possible the materials needed for experiment. Sometimes the library was built above the

13.6 Strathclyde Graduate School, Glasgow, UK, by Reiach and Hall.

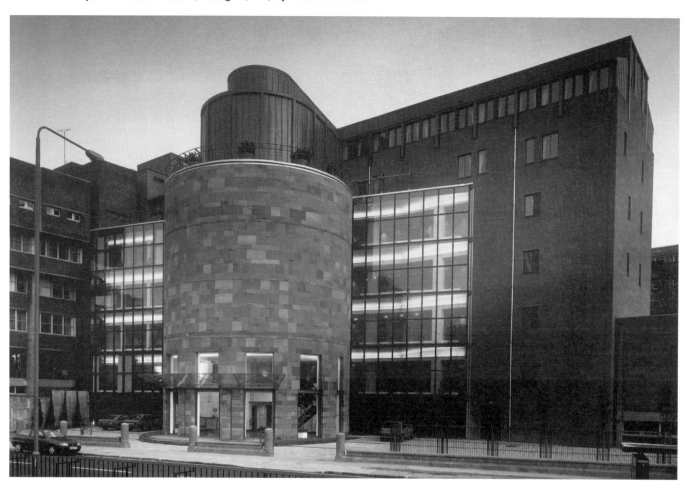

gateway between college vegetable garden and student quad, reminding scholars of the centrality of learning and horticulture to university life. Students were not only expected to study but also to garden. Nature, agriculture, experment and reading were intertwined in almost monastic fasion in the early European universities. Sustainability has, therefore, tentacles throughout history in the university campus.

Building bridges with the community

If buildings exist to help students understand social, ecological and artistic ideals, they are also key elements in building bridges with the wider community. Increasingly campus buildings are made available to the town at large so that the university and city it serves can develop effective partnership. The sports hall, library and lecture theatres are frequently used for study or recreation by those not registered on university courses. As multi-disciplinary, multi-cultural and town/gown links expand, the university becomes a place without walls, an asset for society at large. Here again, the main buildings on campus have a role to play in this interaction: they need to be welcoming, exciting and uplifting. As university education expands to include an ever-broadening audience (nearly 40 per cent of school

leavers currently in the UK) the buildings cease to be the exclusive reserve of a few. They become in effect the learning landscape for a wider clientele: bridges which facilitate the flow of ideas, skills and knowledge in both directions.

New growth, fresh paradigm: four key actions for campus planning

The twentieth century has witnessed an unprecedented expansion in university education. Globally, education is the second fastest growing industry after tourism. New universities are being created in the developed world as former polytechnics and some higher technical colleges are given degree awarding powers. In the emerging world, the creation of universities is seen as essential to global competitiveness and regional development. Existing universities are also enjoying rapid expansion with, in the USA, Germany and Japan, an expectation that a half of all school leavers will become university graduates. Under such pressure how can the paradigms upon which higher education depends survive? These are found not only in the teaching and research programmes but in the buildings on campus and the campus layout itself. If the university is to remain a special place then four key actions must follow:

(a)   First, the briefing and procurement system must recognise the intellectual ambitions of higher education and link building development with the pedagogic ideals which underpin the system. Great architecture – the legacy of nearly a thousand years of campus making – requires enlightened, forward-looking briefs. Too often the second-rate is allowed to happen because of cost-cutting systems such as 'design and build' and PFI (Public Finance Initiative).

(b)   Second, there is the need to recognise the difficult big picture rather than concentrate upon the easier small part. Put another way, it is the importance of urban and landscape design to the campus, as opposed to the specifics of an individual building. Too frequently action is focused upon an element of the campus (usually a new building) without adequate regard being paid to the whole. Good campuses have visually strong and spatially cohesive plans. These, as at Berkeley, Tucson in Arizona, or Birmingham (UK), are imposed as an ordering system at birth. Masterplans, with design codes, are more important than plans articulating only land-use zones. They need to provide for order and growth, for the predictable and unexpected. Too few universities accept the discipline of a three-dimensional plan and gradually pay the price through disorder and chaos. Where universities grow from smaller inner city foundations they still require a framework of urban and landscape discipline. Such 'brownfield' universities (as at the University of Sunderland) need to moderate opportunism with a sense of the long term. Every time a specific new building is under consideration, its effect upon the ensemble as a place of higher learning should be paramount. America, with its tradition of campus masterplans, has much to teach Europe about grasping the big picture.

(c)   Third, campuses should continue to experiment and innovate. Universities are the test beds for new ideas – buildings are no different in this respect to courses, methods of management or research methodologies. Great universities have great buildings, just as the best football teams have the finest stadia and innovative companies the most adventurous workplaces. If a university regards itself as anything more than a teaching machine, then its mission of excellence should be expressed in architecture. Afterall, campus buildings survive for hundreds of years, and far exceed the lifespan of fashions of procurement or vice-chancellors. The agenda of excellence changes over time: the scientific rationalism of Wren in Oxford, the constructional inventiveness of Labrouste in his academic and library buildings in Paris, the orthogonal discipline of Mies van der Rohe at IIT, all engage in their own fashion in a dialogue with space and time. Campuses should remain places of innovation even in the dark ages of budget-cutting building procurement.

(d)   Fourth, universities should be places of ecological design: the re-connection of man and nature through

13.8   Faculty of Design, University of Salford, Manchester, UK, by Hodder Associates.

the vehicle of campus making. Environmental sustainability is the basis for some of the best examples of university architecture. Often evolved with the help of the academics who will occupy the building, these green structures embody the agenda of global warming which university research helped to bring public attention. If universities fail to innovate in the area of sustainability they will miss the opportunity to give students a glimpse into the future. Without a sense of tomorrow, a university is lost. And without a willingness to use buildings to change the world, a university will be turning its back upon a long and honourable sense of history. Sustainability has arguably a taproot through to the medieval college. No place offers a better chance to demonstrate the benefits of green design to the world at large than the university campus.

The campus of the future

It is clear from the examples of best practice cited earlier that universities use good modern architecture as a means of enhancing their competitive edge. This was always the case, but in today's climate of the business orientated university with its eye upon student numbers, the quality of the campus as a physical entity is crucial. If an institution is to attract students and to recruit the best young academic staff then it needs to see design as part of the marketing of an educational service. The campus is a trading floor and the buildings its billboard.

Competitiveness through design leads to architectural innovation in a variety of ways. We have seen how Stanford University has always invested in design talent, employing for its later clinical research building the British architect Lord Foster. His practice has responded not only by creating an appropriate high-tech image to reflect the latest in medical research but also by forming a central glazed street where scientists can meet informally for coffee. This space epitomises the interaction necessary in research but it too rarely finds expression in building briefs. Being casual and flexible of function, such spaces are too easily overlooked, yet without the challenge of academic interface, research can become stifled by the walls of the laboratory.

If high-tech architecture is used to convey a message which is appealing and attractive to the research community, it serves equally well the environment of the learning resource centre. At the Paul Hamlyn library at Thames Valley University, designed by Lord Rogers of Riverside, visually distinctive metallic modern design is used to complement the world of IT learning. Within an embrace of yellow painted curved steel beams, glass and louvres, students discover the benefit of the Internet to higher education. Architecture and the computer are united in projecting an image of openness, imagination and discovery. Computers not only give unprecedented access to knowledge, they amplify the imagination of students and architects alike. The campus of the future needs to reflect this.

Of all the strands of current architecture, high tech seems most appropriate to a progressive university. Through steel, aluminium, glass and photovoltaic panel, it can lure students away from more traditional institutions. You have only to look at the prospectii of universities to realise how much weight they attach to architectural image. And no better advertisement exists for an upwardly mobile university, especially one which grew from a polytechnic or technical institution, than high-technology driven new buildings.

If image matters then the dilemma for a university lies in deciding what kind of message to project. High tech suits many institutions but not all. Cambridge University has seen fads come and go and its tradition is one of college conservatism. When so much depends upon generous donors their taste comes into the aesthetic debate. At Kaetsu College in Cambridge, modern architecture is tempered by a little oriental proportioning and symbolism – itself a response to the Japanese benefactor. At Cambridge's Judge Institute, by the architect John Outram, the new management studies building develops an unique new classical order, what Outram calls his 'robot order', to create a colourful, well proportioned interior for business students. Again, client taste had a say, not in the detailed architectural language, but in the appointment of an architect who was interested in decorated construction.

If multi-culturalism exists in the university architecture at Oxford and Cambridge, and in more carefree guise at Berkeley and Arizona, then where do the many new green campus buildings fit into the scene? In some ways sustainability bridges the two worlds of abstracted placeless high tech and place related vernacular design. The best modern low-energy designs are busy modernising the vernacular and regionalising the modern. Two main directions are evident in the sustainable campus – the adoption of low-energy strategies and the rediscovery of local building traditions. The former, represented by the work of Feilden Clegg at Sunderland and Sir Michael Hopkins and Partners at Nottingham, brings to the buildings qualities which students can use to learn about environmental problems. In the process a new ecological order emerges; one which challenges the globally arrogant modernism from Hong Kong to New York, giving universities relevance as a beacon for the future.

The latter trend is still in a state of formation. The vernacular has always existed on the university campus but a new kind of vernacular is emerging, one which uses wind towers and courtyards to moderate the climate. Green strategies based upon regional climatic traditions are a feature of the new seaside campus of King Faisal University at Dammam in Saudi Arabia, the new engineering building at the University of Cyprus and the Queen's Building at De Montfort University. In each example vernacular traditions are reinterpreted, brought up to date and allowed to influence more orthodox design methodologies. In each too, strong masterplans exist to guide architects from across the generations.

Image, whether high-tech, multi-cultural or green matters to a university. And there is no better way to project an image than through building design. At one level architecture, urban and landscape design are the packaging of a service, at another they are the vehicle whereby inter-generational values are conveyed. For universities with a long lineage, image is already established in stone and concrete, for new universities however, image, is a matter for the fashioning. History teaches that to ignore the power of architecture to communicate cultural value is to miss an opportunity to landmark not only place but time. And when the world's universities are seeking to differentiate themselves to avoid global anonymity there are few better ways to signal the differences between universities than through the medium of building. At no time since the nineteenth century have campuses been such a communicator of image and value.

Image, therefore, matters but it is in conflict with much current procurement wisdom. Building briefs too rarely acknowledge its presence and only occasionally do campus masterplans establish a framework for innovation as against order. The usual path to procurement is that of minimum cost and the elimination of financial or time risk. Yet innovative design, which is fundamental to image, requires

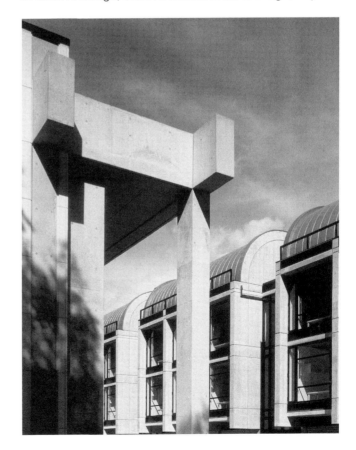

13.9 Kobe Institute, Japan, by Troughton McAslan.

13.10 Innovative low-energy student housing in Northern England by Feilden Clegg. The building acts as a symbol of regeneration for redundant docklands and a shop window for the new University of Sunderland, UK.

extra time for design, additional risk in terms of new technologies, and a higher investment in materials. The usual method of construction is that of 'design and build', or 'prefabrication', or the use of global construction companies who offer a 'package'. As a result innovative methods of building are ignored, regional cultural differences are overlooked, and the benefits of low-risk repetition win over high-risk design complexity. Universities which value 'image' cherish architecture rather than just building. The difference between them is akin to the distinction made in universities between learning and teaching – the first requires a strategy of intellectual investment, the second merely a good memory. The architecture of the campus is as much an investment in the academic programme as the books, and without the pursuit of inquiry through good new design, a university will fail to compete as a global player.

Bibliography

SELECTED BIBLIOGRAPHY

Tony Birks, *Building the New Universities,* David and Charles (1972), Newton Abbot.

Richard P Dober, *Campus Planning,* Reinhold Publishing Corporation (1963), New York.

Richard P Dober, *Campus Architecture: Buildings in Groves of Academe*, McGraw-Hill (1996), New York.

A Peter Fawcett and Neil Jackson, *Campus Critique: The Architecture of the University of Nottingham*, University of Nottingham Press (1998), Nottingham.

A J Metric Handbook, 'Higher Education', especially Chapter 31, pp 264–273, Architectural Press (1976), Oxford.

Neufert Architects' Data, BSP Professional Books, Oxford, 1994 edition, especially chapter on 'Colleges' pp. 134–142.

Godfrey Thompson, *Planning and Design of Library Buildings* (Third Edition), Butterworth Architecture (1989), Oxford.

Paul V Turner, *Campus: An American Planning Tradition*, MIT Press (1984), Cambridge, Mass.

Richard G Wilson and Sara A Butler, *University of Virginia: An Architectural Tour*, Princeton Architectural Press (1998), Princeton.

JOURNALS

Various consulted, in particular: *The Architectural Review*, *The Architects' Journal*, *Architecture Today*, *World Architecture*, *Architectural Record*, *Bauwelt*, *Japan Architect*, *Architectural Design*, *RIBA Journal* and *Architectural Forum*.

Illustration acknowledgements

The author and publisher would like to thank the following individuals and organisations for permission to reproduce material. We have made every effort to contact and acknowledge copyright holders, but if any errors have been made we would be happy to correct them at a later printing.

Abbey Holford Rowe **24**
Ahrends, Burton and Koralek 11.5
Alan Forbes 13.6
Alvar Aalto Foundation 9.5
Austin: Smith-Lord 12.12
Balliol College, Oxford 12.11
Basil Spence and Partners 3.5, **15**
Beeah Architects 1.6, 2.7, 2.8
Bennetts Associates 10.6
British Library 4.23, 13.1
Building Design Partnership 4.29, 5.3, 7.10
Corrigan, Soundy Kilaiditi Associates 12.3
Dennis Gilbert / View 13.4, 13.8, **11**, **12**, **17**
Edward Cullinan Associates 4.20
Feilden Clegg 12.15, 13.10, **14**
Foster and Partners 7.6, 7.9, 8.8, 8.12, 8.14, 8.15, **6**
Frank Gehry 10.3
GRM Kennedy and Partners 6.2
HKPA 1.9
Hodder Associates 10.7
HOK 1.11
Howard Bingham / Abbey Holford Rowe 9.11
James H. Morris / Foster and Partners 7.7, 7.8
James Stirling Foundation 1.2, 8.4
Jeremy Dixon 12.10
Jeremy Dixon / Edward Jones 8.16, 12.7, **7**
John Andrews 1.10
John McAslan and Partners 3.8, 11.2, 13.9, **8**, **13**
John Outram 11.7
Jourda and Perraudin 8.9, 9.8, 10.4, **5**
Katsuhisa Kid **18**
Katsuhisa Kid / Richard Rogers Partnership 1.5, **4**

Kochi University 4.31, 4.34, 13.7
Kouvo and Partanen 10.1
MacCormac, Jamieson, Prichard 2.9, 12.1, 12.4, 12.5
Mario Cucinella with Andreas Kyprianou 5.7
Martin Bates **3**
Martine Hamilton-Knight 13.2, **16**, **22**
Michael Hopkins and Partners 5.5, 5.6, 11.3
Michael Wilford and Partners 1.4, 2.5, 2.6, 4.6, 7.4, 9.4, 9.6, **19**, **26**
National Library of Scotland 13.5
New York University 7.3
Nicholas Grimshaw and Partners 8.13, 9.10
Nicholas Ray Associates 12.13
Ohio State University 2.3, 3.2, 4.8, 4.15, 9.1, 9.2
ORMS Architects 11.6
Peter Durant 12.6, 12.14
Peter Durant / MacCormac, Jamieson, Prichard 7.15, **27**
Pondicherry University 4.16
Reiach and Hall 8.6, 8.10, 8.11
Rem Koolhaus / OMA 9.7
Richard Bryant / Arcaid 7.16, **9**, **10**
Richard Rogers Partnership 7.14
Rick Mather 5.1, 11.4
RMJM 1.12, 1.14, 2.4, 2.10, 3.7, 4.32, 4.33, 11.1, **20**
Sasaki Associates and Michael Dennis Associates 1.16, 3.3
SJV Stirling Council 1.8
Skidmore, Owings and Merrill 1.13, 4.17
Stanford University 1.3
Strathclyde University 12.9
UCD 4.18
University of British Columbia 1.15, 2.2, 3.1, 4.1, 4.2, 4.3, 4.9, 4.14, 4.24
University of Michigan 1.7, 2.1, 4.12, 4.13, 10.2
University of Pennsylvania 12.8
University of Sussex 3.4
University of Virginia 1.19, 1.20
Yale University 1.21

Figure numbers in **bold** indicate colour illustrations.

Index